A
"*Wonderful*"
Deception

A
"Wonderful"
Deception

The Further New Age Implications
of the Emerging Purpose Driven Movement

Warren Smith

Lighthouse Trails Publishing
Silverton, Oregon

Library of Congress Cataloging-in-Publication Data

Smith, Warren, M.S.W.
  A "wonderful" deception : the further new age implications of the emerging purpose driven movement / Warren Smith.
      p. cm.
  Includes bibliographical references.
  ISBN 978-0-9824881-0-2 (softbound : alk. paper)
  1. Christianity and other religions~New Age movement. 2. Warren, Richard, 1954- Purpose-driven life. I. Title.
  BR128.N48S65 2009
  248.4~dc22
                          2009021204

Contents

A wonderful and horrible thing is committed in the land; The prophets prophesy falsely, and the priests bear rule by their means; and my people love to have it so: and what will ye do in the end thereof?

—Jeremiah 5:30-31

Preface

We are admonished in Scripture to speak the truth in love (Ephesians 4:15). We are also told to "reprove, rebuke, exhort with all longsuffering and doctrine" (2 Timothy 4:2). Hopefully, it is in this light that I convey my concerns regarding Rick Warren and his Purpose Driven movement.

I would not be writing this book if Rick Warren were just another neighborhood preacher. But when a pastor sells thirty million books, is the founder of a 162-nation network, has trained over "400,000 ministers and priests" throughout the world,[1] and presents his movement as the "Intel chip" for and the "Windows system" of the 21st century church,[2] it becomes imperative to search the Scriptures to see if what he is teaching is really so (Acts 17:11). We are not to blindly follow spiritual leaders just because they are in a position of leadership and power. We must be true to Scripture and to our Lord and Savior Jesus Christ.

By the mid 1990s, the church was led to believe that the New Age had peaked and was no longer a serious threat. In reality, New Age teachings were spreading exponentially in almost every conceivable way. Many of us who were formerly in the New Age could see this clearly. The New Age had become mainstream and was already in the process of reinventing itself as the "New Spirituality."

Today, this New Age/New Spirituality is the spiritual foundation for an emerging "new worldview" that if adopted by the world—and the church—could usher in a false world peace that in actuality will be no *real* peace at all. It will be a deceptive New Age peace for a deceptive New Age. It will be everything that the true Jesus Christ warned would come in His name.

In 2002, I authored *Reinventing Jesus Christ: The New Gospel*. In that book, I explain how the New Age is much more deceptive and all-encompassing than what is being presented to the church by today's church leaders. In a chapter titled "The Silent Church," I describe how the church seems to be walking into a spiritual trap. I ask why Christian leaders aren't warning believers about the New Age/New Spirituality, which is working its way into the church. Rick Warren's best-selling book, *The Purpose Driven Life* gave me my answer: The reason Christian leaders aren't taking the New Age more seriously is because figures, like Warren, are not *ringing out* a warning and are themselves being influenced and deceived by the New Age.

A whole new wave of church leaders is overtaking the church. But rather than declaring "all the counsel of God" and warning about spiritual deception, the focus of these leaders is almost entirely on the culture and on fulfilling "God's Dream"— a concept that Robert Schuller has been popularizing for over thirty-five years. "God's Dream" is an unbiblical concept that is being embraced by countless numbers of Christian and New Age leaders alike.

I have been warning about New Age teachings since the day of my conversion in 1984. It has never been my intention or desire to critique men who present themselves as Christian leaders. However, as the church has become more and more intersected with the New Age, I am compelled by the Lord to speak up and warn against the very spirituality the Lord delivered me from. In Matthew 24:3-5, Jesus warns that spiritual deception will be the predominant sign before His return. That deception is happening right now.

In Jeremiah 9:3, Jeremiah warns about those who are "not valiant for the truth." Sadly, Rick Warren is a man who is not wholly valiant for the truth. For whatever reasons, he does not declare "all" the counsel of God (Acts 20:27) and he does not seriously reprove and expose the New Age/New Spirituality that is so clearly in our midst (Ephesians 5:13). It is a pastor's job to protect the flock from heresy, and Rick Warren is not doing that. On the contrary, his worldwide movement has serious New Age implications.

It is important and very necessary to do good works. We *should* help the poor, feed the hungry, and care for the sick, the widows, and the orphans. But we cannot, and we must not, water down or change the teachings of the Bible in the process.

I have done my best to describe some of the further New Age implications of the emerging Purpose Driven movement. I now present these concerns to you.

> Consider what I say; and the Lord give thee understanding in all things. (2 Timothy 2:7)

Warren Smith
April 2009

Introduction

The thing that hath been, it is that which shall be;
and that which is done is that which shall be done:
and there is no new thing under the sun.

— Ecclesiastes 1:9

I was still writing this book, *A "Wonderful" Deception,* when Rick Warren's public relations firm announced that the Purpose Driven pastor was forming an "extensive" publishing partnership with Reader's Digest Association, Inc.[1] I had already completed several chapters that describe how New Age sympathizers Norman Vincent Peale and Robert H. Schuller inspired and helped to create the Church Growth movement—a movement that subtly and not so subtly evolved from Peale's "Positive thinking" to Schuller's "Possibility thinking" to Rick Warren's "Purpose Driven" thinking.

Thus, I was not surprised when I discovered that DeWitt Wallace, the late founder and longtime Executive Director of Reader's Digest Association Inc., was "a good friend" of Norman Vincent Peale[2] and that *Reader's Digest* magazine had faithfully published Peale's articles for nearly forty years—from the late 1940s to the late 1980s.[3] Therefore it seemed almost fitting that Reader's Digest Association was now going to publish Rick Warren's new *Purpose Driven Connection* magazine.

When I first heard about Rick Warren's partnership with Reader's Digest, my mind immediately flashed back through the years to a personal memory. In 1967, after graduating from the University of Pennsylvania, and in the midst of the Vietnam War,

I found myself in Army basic training at Fort Dix, New Jersey. When I finished my basic training, chances were high that I would be shipped off to Vietnam. But instead of receiving orders for Vietnam, I was assigned to the White House in Washington DC. To my amazement, I would be living in my own apartment and working directly for the President of the United States.

After obtaining a top-security clearance, I began my new assignment with the White House Communications Agency. The agency was responsible for providing communications support to the President and Vice President wherever they traveled or happened to be. While many of my more technically-skilled colleagues traveled with the President and Vice-President around the country and abroad, my less technical supply job usually kept me bound to the DC area. In fact, during my entire two years with the White House Communications Agency, there was only one time that I ever made an outside trip with the President. Forty years ago, I was part of the White House advance team that prepared the way for President Richard Nixon's visit to his friend DeWitt Wallace of *Reader's Digest* magazine.[4]

The world is fond of saying that "there is a reason for everything" and that "what goes around comes around." I don't really know what to say about that presidential visit I took to the heart of *Reader's Digest* country so many years ago. But I remember the New York Hudson Valley hamlet that DeWitt Wallace and *Reader's Digest* called home like it was yesterday. What irony that the only trip I took on behalf of the President of the United States was to the founder and Executive Director of *Reader's Digest*. And how fitting that the same Readers Digest Association Inc. that formerly published the writings and teachings of Robert Schuller's mentor Norman Vincent Peale has begun publishing the writings and teachings of Rick Warren.[5]

Rick Warren describes himself as a "change agent,"[6] but the more he appears to change things the more things seem to remain the same. *Reader's Digest* successfully promoted Norman Vincent Peale's books and articles and kept Peale's ministry in the world's limelight for nearly four decades. What worked for Peale then will surely work for Rick Warren now.

As I will later describe in this book, Norman Vincent Peale's strong New Age sympathies came to my attention after *Deceived on Purpose* was published in 2004. Shortly thereafter, I would learn of Peale's New Age influence on Robert Schuller and its subsequent impact on the Church Growth movement that includes Rick Warren today.

However, before we look at some of the further New Age implications of the emerging Purpose Driven movement, let us first review some of the original New Age implications described in *Deceived on Purpose*.

One

Deceived on Purpose

A little leaven leaveneth the whole lump.

—Galatians 5:9

I was working as a hospice social worker on the California coast in the late summer of 2003 when I first read Rick Warren's book *The Purpose Driven Life*. Having been formerly involved in the New Age movement, I immediately recognized some serious New Age implications to Warren's Purpose Driven movement. Feeling compelled to warn the church about the spiritual confusion that could result from some of his teachings, I resigned my hospice job to write *Deceived on Purpose: The New Age Implications of the Purpose Driven Church*. The book was published in August of 2004.

In *Deceived on Purpose*, while I did not describe Rick Warren or his Purpose Driven Church as "New Age," I did point out the many New Age implications regarding his teachings and the danger those teachings posed for the church.

Because Saddleback apologists have misrepresented these warnings and because my concerns have grown significantly since I wrote *Deceived on Purpose*, I have written this follow-up book. To lay a proper foundation for A *"Wonderful" Deception*, I will briefly summarize some of the basic concerns I expressed in *Deceived on Purpose*. I will recap these in the remainder of this first chapter.

Ten Basic Concerns

1) Rick Warren Cites New Age Leader

In *The Purpose Driven Life*, Rick Warren introduces his main themes of "hope" and "purpose." Inexplicably, Warren chooses to introduce "hope" and "purpose" in his book by citing Dr. Bernie Siegel—a veteran New Age leader who claims to have a spirit-guide named George.[1] Somehow, readers of *The Purpose Driven Life* are expected to believe that God inspired Warren to introduce the themes of hope and purpose by referencing the "wisdom" of Bernie Siegel, an author and leader in the New Age movement. But the Bible warns that this kind of worldly wisdom is not from God and can confuse and stumble believers, and completely mislead unbelievers:

> This wisdom descendeth not from above, but is earthly, sensual, devilish. (James 3:15)

> Let us not therefore judge one another any more: but judge this rather, that no man put a stumbling block or an occasion to fall in his brother's way. (Romans 14:13)

2) Rick Warren Sends Confusing New Age Message: "God is in everything"

Out of the fifteen different Bible versions Rick Warren uses in *The Purpose Driven Life*, he chooses to cite Ephesians 4:6 from a new translation that erroneously conveys the panentheistic New Age teaching that God is "in" everything. According to New Age leaders, this teaching is foundational to the New Age/New Spirituality.[2] Yet of these fifteen Bible versions Warren uses in his book, he chooses the *New Century Version* that has potentially misled millions of Purpose Driven readers to believe this key New Age doctrine that God is "in" everything. Regarding God, Warren writes:

The Bible says, *"He rules everything and is everywhere and is in everything"*[3]

The *New Century Version* quoted by Rick Warren verbalizes what *A Course in Miracles* and my other New Age books taught me years ago—that God is "in" everyone and everything. This completely misrepresents what the apostle Paul is saying in Ephesians 4:6. In *Deceived on Purpose*, I explain:

> In this Scripture Paul is not writing to the world at large. The book of Ephesians is Paul's letter to the Church of Ephesus and to the faithful followers of Jesus Christ. In Ephesians 1:1 he makes it clear that he is writing to "the saints which are at Ephesus, and to the faithful in Christ Jesus."

According to properly translated Scripture, God is not "in" everyone and everything, and God's Holy Spirit *only* indwells those who truly accept Jesus Christ as their Lord and Savior (John 14:15-17; Acts 5:32). In *Deceived on Purpose*, I wrote:

> Because the Church of Ephesus was composed of believers who had accepted Jesus as their Lord and Savior, God had sent His Holy Spirit to them. Therefore, as a result of their conversion God's Holy Spirit resided in them all. Thus, Paul is *only* addressing the *believers* of Ephesus and the "faithful in Christ Jesus" when he stated that God is "above all, and through all, and in *you* all" (emphasis added). He was not saying that God is present in unbelievers. He was not saying that God is "in" everyone and "in" everything. That is what the New Age teaches.[4]

It is vital to understand the difference in renderings of Ephesians 4:6. Compare the *New Century Version* that Rick Warren quotes with the *King James Bible*:

He rules everything and is everywhere and is in everything. (NCV)

One God and Father of all, who is above all, and through all, and in you all. (*KJV*)

3) Rick Warren and *The Message*

In *The Purpose Driven Life*, Rick Warren cites Eugene Peterson's *The Message* more than any other Bible version. *The Message* is laden with its own set of questionable New Age implications. In the first chapter of *The Purpose Driven Life*, five of the six Scriptures Warren cites come from *The Message*. Warren states that *The Message* is a Bible "paraphrase," yet he frequently writes, "the Bible says" when quoting from *The Message*.[5]

One of the many examples of the New Age implications of *The Message* is seen in Eugene Peterson's paraphrasing of the Lord's Prayer. Where most translations read "in earth, as it is in heaven," Peterson inserts the occult/New Age phrase "as above, so below." The significance of this mystical occult saying is seen clearly in *As Above, So Below*, a book published in 1992 by the editors of *New Age Journal*. Chief editor Ronald S. Miller describes how the occult/magical saying "as above, so below" conveys the "fundamental truth about the universe"—the teaching that "we are all one" because God is "immanent" or "within" everyone and everything. Miller writes:

Thousands of years ago in ancient Egypt, the great master alchemist Hermes Trismegistus, believed to be a contemporary of the Hebrew prophet Abraham, proclaimed this fundamental truth about the universe: "As above, so below; as below, so above." This maxim implies that the transcendent God beyond the physical universe and the immanent God within ourselves are one. Heaven and Earth, spirit and matter, the invisible and the visible worlds form a unity to which we are intimately linked.[6]

Miller continues describing the meaning of "as above, so below" by quoting Sufi scholar Reshad Field:

> "'As above, so below' means that the two worlds are instantaneously seen to be one when we realize our essential unity with God. . . . The One and the many, time and eternity, are all One."[7] (ellipsis in original)

In 2004 when I searched "as above, so below" on the Internet, the first entry listed further defined this "key" New Age term:

> This phrase comes from the beginning of The Emerald Tablet and embraces the entire system of traditional and modern magic which was inscribed upon the tablet in cryptic wording by Hermes Trismegistus. The significance of this phrase is that it is believed to hold the key to all mysteries. All systems of magic are claimed to function by this formula. "'That which is above is the same as that which is below' . . . The universe is the same as God, God is the same as man."[8]

Most of the references, either on websites or in books and magazines containing the phrase "as above, so below" describe the term as having the same occult/mystical/New Age/esoteric/magical sources. One website states:

> This ancient phrase, "As above, so below" describes the Oneness of All That Is.[9]

In *Deceived on Purpose*, I discuss my concerns over Rick Warren placing such great emphasis on Eugene Peterson's *The Message*. When I looked up Ephesians 4:6 in *The Message*, Peterson's paraphrase (like the *New Century Version*) also definitely lends itself to the New Age interpretation that God is present "in" everyone. In *The Message*, Peterson introduces his readers—with no parenthetical warnings or explanations—to the concept of 'Oneness':

> You have one Master, one faith, one baptism, one God and Father of all, who rules over all, works through all, and is present in all. Everything you are and think and do is permeated with Oneness.[10]

The "as above, so below" God "in" everything "Oneness" message of Eugene Peterson's paraphrase *The Message* sounds strikingly similar to the same "as above, so below" God "in" everything "Oneness" message of the New Age/New Spirituality. Such a teaching is contrary to what the Bible teaches. We are only "one" in Christ Jesus when we repent of our sins and accept Him as our Lord and Savior. Galatians 3:26-28 states:

> For ye are all the children of God by faith in Christ Jesus. For as many of you as have been baptized into Christ have put on Christ. There is neither Jew nor Greek, there is neither bond nor free, there is neither male nor female: for ye are all one *in Christ Jesus*. (emphasis added)

4) The *Purpose Driven Life's* Distorted View of Bible Prophecy

In *The Purpose Driven Life*, Rick Warren strongly discourages the study of prophecy. He states that "in essence" Jesus told his disciples: "The details of my return are none of your business."[11] Contrary to what Warren writes, in Jesus' discussion on the Mount of Olives, He tells His disciples that an understanding of the details of His return is very important. He provides much needed prophetic information so that His followers will not be deceived about the details of His return at the end of time. In *Deceived on Purpose*, I explain:

> He warns that there will be false teachers and false teachings that will try to confuse the details of His return. He provides the prophetic detail because He didn't want His disciples, or any of us, mistaking Antichrist's arrival for His own return. He initiates His lengthy prophetic discourse by saying, "Take heed that no man deceive you." He ends His discussion by warning them to "watch" and "be ready."[12]

As someone who has come out of New Age teachings, I find it very disturbing that Rick Warren writes that the details of Jesus' return are none of our business. In *Deceived on Purpose*, I talk about the role that these details had in my own eventual conversion:

> Understanding the events surrounding His return was critical to understanding how badly I had been deceived by my New Age teachings. I had learned from reading the Bible that there is a false Christ on the horizon and that for a number of years I had unknowingly been one of his followers. Because the Bible's clear authoritative teachings about the real Jesus and His true return had been brought to my attention, I was able to see how deceived I was. By understanding that there is a false Christ trying to counterfeit the true Christ's return, I was able to renounce the false Christ I had been following and commit my life to the true Jesus Christ.[13]

5) Rick Warren and John Marks Templeton

Rick Warren unwittingly lent himself to the "purposes" of New Age sympathizer John Marks Templeton, as shown in *Deceived on Purpose*:

> Even as I write, [New Age leader] Neale Donald
> Walsch's New Age colleague Wayne Dyer is
> teaching the principles of the New Spirituality
> to an unsuspecting American public on a 3-hour
> PBS television special. His subject? The power of
> intention and purpose. While Dyer was cleverly
> presenting the New Spirituality by talking
> about the power of "purpose," Rick Warren
> was judging a "Power of Purpose" essay contest
> for the New Age-based Templeton Foundation.
> John Templeton—with his strong New Age and
> metaphysical leanings—believes in a "shared
> divinity between God and humanity."[14]

I pointed out that the late Templeton had been featured on
the cover of Robert Schuller's *Possibilities* magazine and was described as "my wonderful role model" by Neale Donald Walsch.

6) Robert Schuller's Influence on Rick Warren

I discovered that Rick Warren had been greatly influenced by
Robert Schuller and that he frequently used unattributed mate-
rial from Schuller's writings. In promoting his 2004 Robert H.
Schuller Institute for Successful Church Leadership, Schuller
stated that Warren was a graduate of his Institute.[15] Furthermore,
on an April 4, 2004 *Hour of Power* television broadcast, Schuller
described how Warren had come to his Institute for Successful
Church Leadership "time after time."[16] And Rick Warren's wife,
Kay, was quoted in a 2002 *Christianity Today* article saying that
Schuller "had a profound influence on Rick."[17]

In reading Schuller's past writings, it soon became apparent
that Schuller had indeed greatly influenced Rick Warren's ministry and that Warren often used Schuller's material without any
attribution to Schuller.

One of the many examples where Warren emulates Schuller's material can be seen in the following comparison of their
writings. In his 1982 book *Self-Esteem: The New Reformation*,

Robert Schuller writes:

> Our very survival "as a species depends on hope. And without hope we will lose the faith that we can cope."[18]

Twenty years later in his 2002 book *The Purpose Driven Life*, Rick Warren writes:

> Hope is as essential to your life as air and water. You need hope to cope.[19]

Another example of how Rick Warren mirrors Robert Schuller is found in Warren's 1995 book *The Purpose Driven Church*. He concludes his book by writing:

> Accept the challenge of becoming a purpose-driven church! The greatest churches in history are yet to be built.[20]

Rick Warren's statement is almost a direct quote from Schuller's 1986 book *Your Church Has A Fantastic Future!*, which quotes a pastor saying:

> Ten years ago, I heard Dr. Robert Schuller say at his leadership conference, "The greatest churches in the world are yet to be built!"[21]

These are just two of many other examples I found where Rick Warren uses unattributed material from Schuller's writings and teachings. In *Deceived on Purpose*, I wrote:

> The more I read Robert Schuller, the more I was shocked at how so many of Rick Warren's thoughts, ideas, references, words, terms, phrases, and quotes in *The Purpose Driven Life* seemed to be directly inspired by Schuller's writings and teachings.[22]

7) Rick Warren and Robert Schuller's "New Reformation" & "God's Dream"

Rick Warren's proposed "New Reformation" and his "God's Dream" Global P.E.A.C.E. Plan are strikingly similar to Robert Schuller's proposed "New Reformation" and his "God's Dream" plan "to redeem society." The only real difference between their basic plans is that Schuller proposed his "New Reformation" and "God's Dream" plan twenty years previous to Warren. In his 1982 book *Self-Esteem: The New Reformation*, Schuller called for a "New Reformation" in the church.[23] To accomplish this New Reformation he frequently invoked the metaphor "God's Dream" to describe God's "great plan to redeem society."[24] Twenty years later, Warren was also calling for a "New Reformation" in the church.[25] To accomplish his proposed New Reformation, Warren also invoked the "God's Dream" metaphor that Schuller had used over two decades earlier to describe his New Reformation and his "plan."[26] Warren described his new reformational P.E.A.C.E. Plan as "God's Dream For You—And The World!,"[27] which also happens to resemble the PEACE Plan proposed by Neale Donald Walsch.

In *Deceived on Purpose*, I wrote:

> Following Schuller's forty-year commitment to his church, Rick Warren made a forty-year commitment to the Saddleback community. He "grew" his mega-church by faithfully implementing all that he had learned from Schuller. . . . Now Schuller's concept of "God's Dream" was being used to inspire millions of Christians to get behind his [Warren's] 5-Step P.E.A.C.E. Plan to "change the world"—a 5-Step P.E.A.C.E. Plan that, on paper, bore an eerie resemblance to the 5-Step PEACE Plan proposed by Neale Donald Walsch and his New Age "God."[28]

8) New Age Embraces Schuller's New Reformation

In Neale Donald Walsch's 2002 book, *The New Revelations*, Walsch and his New Age "God" praise Robert Schuller's ministry and laud Schuller's call for a New Reformation. Walsch describes how he and his "God" are also calling for a "New Reformation." In fact, they commend Schuller and believe that Schuller's New Reformation can merge with their plan to help bridge the divide between the Christian church and the teachings of the New Age/New Spirituality. They also present their New Reformation in the form of a 5-Step PEACE Plan[29] that is similarly put forth in the form of an acronym—much like Rick Warren's 5-Step P.E.A.C.E. Plan.[30] In *The New Revelations: A Conversation with God*, Walsch, in a conversation with his "God," states:

> Rev. Robert H. Schuller, the American Christian minister who founded the famous Crystal Cathedral in Garden Grove, California, said twenty years ago in his book *Self-Esteem: The New Reformation* that what is needed is a second reformation within the Church, to move it away from its message of fear and guilt, retribution, and damnation, and toward a theology of self-esteem.[31]

Walsch quotes Schuller as saying that the "church" is "failing at the deepest level to generate within human beings that quality of personality that can result in the kinds of persons that would make our world a safe and sane society."[32] Walsch continues his conversation with "God" about Robert Schuller:

> Dr. Schuller went on to suggest that "sincere Christians and church-persons can find a theological launching point of universal agreement if they can agree on the universal right and uncompromising need of every person to be treated with great respect simply because he or she is a human being!"[33]

Walsch then calls Schuller an "extraordinary minister" and quotes him again as saying:

> "As a Christian, a theologian, and a churchman within the Reformed tradition, I must believe that it is possible for the church to exist even though it may be in serious error in substance, strategy, style or spirit."[34]

Walsch adds:

> But, he [Schuller] said, ultimately "theologians must have their international, universal, transcreedal, transcultural, transracial standard."[35]

Walsch's "God" answers Walsch:

> Rev. Schuller was profoundly astute in his observations and incredibly courageous in making them public. *I hope he is proud of himself!*
>
> I suggest that such an international, universal, transcreedal, transcultural, transracial standard for theology is the statement: "We Are All One. Ours is not a better way, ours is merely another way."
>
> This can be the gospel of a New Spirituality. It can be a kind of spirituality that gives people back to themselves.[36]

I do not believe it is just coincidence that Neale Donald Walsch—like Robert Schuller and Rick Warren—is also calling for a New Reformation. Nor do I believe it is a coincidence that Walsch and his "God" identify with Schuller and suggest Schuller's New Reformation as a prototype for their PEACE Plan. Nor do I believe it is a coincidence that Warren has also used Schuller's New Reformation as the prototype for *his* P.E.A.C.E. Plan and that both the New Age and Warren have devised 5-Step PEACE Plans to encourage their mutual calls for a New Reformation.

Other New Age leaders, like Bernie Siegel and Gerald Jampolsky also praise Robert Schuller and endorse his writings and teachings.[37] Jampolsky and Schuller have mutually endorsed each other's books.[38] In his book *Self-Esteem: The New Reformation*, Schuller favorably cites Jampolsky and praises the New Age leader for his "profound theology."[39] Yet it is Jampolsky who first introduced me to the teachings of *A Course in Miracles* when I was in the New Age movement. I would later discover to my amazement that *A Course in Miracle* groups were meeting on the grounds of Schuller's Crystal Cathedral back in 1985.[40] I would also learn that Schuller has had an ongoing relationship with his "dear friend" Gerald Jampolsky from the early 1980s up through the present day.[41] And it is not surprising that Bernie Siegel—the New Age leader Rick Warren cites in *The Purpose Driven Life*—had been a long-time member of the Board of Advisors for Jampolsky's *A Course in Miracles*-based New Age Attitudinal Healing Centers.[42]

9) The Implications of Schuller's Influence on Rick Warren

It became evident to me that Rick Warren was incorporating Robert Schuller's plans and teachings into the Evangelical church. Whether it is "God's Dream," God "in" everything, the "New Reformation," or something else, the non-referenced writings and teachings of Robert Schuller have been gradually introduced into the Evangelical church through Rick Warren. In *Deceived on Purpose*, I wrote:

> [I]t seemed that one of Rick Warren's unstated purposes was to mainstream Robert Schuller's teachings into the more traditional "Bible-based" wing of the Church. Many believers who seem to trust Rick Warren, ironically, do not trust Robert Schuller. Rick Warren's "magic" seems to be able to

make the teachings of Robert Schuller palatable to believers who would have otherwise never accepted these same teachings had they come directly from Schuller himself.[43]

Recognizing the overwhelming influence that Robert Schuller has had on Rick Warren and thousands of other pastors, I explain in *Deceived on Purpose* that "The Purpose Driven Church campaign to enlist every man, woman and child into its ranks to 'do' the P.E.A.C.E. Plan and to 'do' God's Dream did not have its origins at Saddleback Church or in the singly inspired mind of Rick Warren."[44] The spiritual foundation of the Purpose Driven movement can be found in the writings and teachings of Schuller's fifty-year ministry. While Warren and other Christian leaders and organizations "forge new Purpose-Driven alliances around the world, the real architect of this seemingly unsinkable Purpose-Driven ship sits quietly in his office at the Crystal Cathedral."[45]

I found it very ironic that while evangelical pastors were studying and speaking at Schuller's Institute for Successful Church Leadership, *A Course in Miracles* groups were also meeting in Crystal Cathedral classrooms. Apparently, these pastors "thought that Schuller knew what he was doing because he had a big 'successful' church, and they wanted one, too."[46]

10) A Serious Concern—A Sober Warning

I concluded *Deceived on Purpose* by stressing that it is not too late for Rick Warren to recognize how he has been influenced by Robert Schuller and by New Age teachings that are taking the church into the New Spirituality. I wrote:

> He [Warren] could open many people's eyes if he started to expose the differences between biblical Christianity and the deceptive teachings of the New Age and its New Spirituality.[47]

However, I presented a sober warning regarding Rick Warren and other Christian leaders who remain in denial about the very real threat of this pervasive spiritual deception that will seriously endanger many who are trusting in their judgment. I explained:

> Sadly, if Rick Warren and other Christian leaders fall for New Age schemes and devices rather than exposing them, they will take countless numbers of sincere people down with them. It will be the blind leading the blind, as they fall further and further into the deceptive ditch of the New Age and its New Spirituality. Undiscerning Christians, who think they are on "the narrow way" preparing the way for Jesus Christ, may discover too late that they had actually been on "the broad way" preparing the way for Antichrist. It is not too late to warn everyone, but it must be done soon before the deception advances any further.[48]

It's Not About Rick Warren

When *Deceived on Purpose* was published in August 2004, I knew the book would be controversial. The New Age implications I had discussed—particularly in regard to Robert Schuller's influence on Rick Warren—had not to my knowledge been raised before. As I stated in *Deceived on Purpose*, my concerns were not personal issues (Matthew 18) between Rick Warren and myself. Because Warren's book was in the public arena and had been sold and distributed to millions of people, I was approaching Warren and his readers in that same public arena. I wrote my comments respectfully and backed them with Scripture and primary source material. In his previous book *The Purpose Driven Church*, Warren had written, "I try to learn from critics."[49] Therefore, I hoped he would seriously consider the New Age implications I had brought out regarding his Purpose Driven movement. Would he begin to see what the New Age was really doing? Would he make some adjustments in the way he was presenting things? Would he recognize the necessity to protect the church from the New Age/New Spirituality?

Ultimately, *Deceived on Purpose* wasn't about Rick Warren. It was about the schemes of our spiritual adversary—an adversary that the Bible refers to as Satan and "the god of this world" (2 Corinthians 4:4). It was about how this adversary uses undiscerning church leaders like Robert Schuller, Rick Warren, and others to further his cunningly devised New Age/New Spirituality. But would Warren and his Saddleback staff recognize how they were being used? And what would be their response—if any—to my book? After *Deceived on Purpose* was released, it didn't take long to get my answers.

Two

Saddleback Responds

> There is no question that Robert Schuller has been
> an influence on Rick through the years.[1]
>
> —Gilbert Thurston, former Saddleback apologist

When *Deceived on Purpose* was first published in August 2004, it created considerable controversy as it suggested there were serious New Age implications to Rick Warren's Purpose Driven movement. Was Warren being deceived on some of his own purposes? Was he—wittingly or unwittingly—leading the church into a New Age/New Spirituality?

Soon after my book was published, Rick Warren's Saddleback Church was questioned about some of the concerns I had written about in my book. People were suddenly taking a closer look at this popular California pastor and his Purpose Driven movement. Many believers were demanding answers from their pastors: *What is going on? Are there actually New Age implications to Rick Warren's Purpose Driven movement? Hasn't the New Age gone away?* These pastors were then contacting Saddleback for some kind of response. *What should we tell people who are asking all these questions?*

The Saddleback Apologists

After a number of months, it came to my attention that a pastor from Winston, Oregon had e-mailed the Saddleback pastoral staff regarding my book.[2] Someone in his church had read *Deceived on Purpose* and was asking questions about Rick Warren that he couldn't answer. In his e-mail to the Saddleback staff, the pastor expressed his unqualified support of Saddleback Church and then asked if Saddleback had developed a response to my book. The pastor received the following e-mail from Saddleback staff member Dan Hurst, who stated:

> This is something that has been taken on by a member of our staff. One of our team members, Gil Thurston has written a response. Attached is his response to the book. It should answer most if not all of the questions you are wondering about.[3]

The attachment Hurst was referring to was a report written by a Saddleback staff member named Gilbert Thurston. It was titled "Response to *Deceived on Purpose* by Warren Smith." Apparently, this report was Saddleback's initial reply to people making inquiries. While the report appeared to answer most of the questions about my book, it really did not. It was very misleading as it consistently misrepresented and minimized the issues I had raised. For a short period of time, the report seemed to be the standard Saddleback response to those who had questions about *Deceived on Purpose*.

Although Gilbert Thurston's "Response to *Deceived on Purpose* by Warren Smith" was an obvious attempt to refute and discredit my concerns, it was not in any way accusatory or mean-spirited. Gilbert Thurston's tone was generally congenial. In fact, he opened his report by stating that *Deceived on Purpose* was "filled with many wonderful teachings on what New Agers believe that will arm us in our fight against the attacks of the enemy."[4] He concluded his paper by saying: "Let me again say that I thank Mr. Smith for his work in educating people in the dangers of New Age."[5] He stated that he was "a better equipped Christian"[6] from having read my book. But apparently, Gilbert Thurston's report was not hard-hitting enough. Soon another apologist arose who was much less kind than Thurston. This new apologist, Richard Abanes, quickly characterized my book as "one of the worst 'apologetic' related books to ever gain popularity in the Christian community."[7] His "take-no-prisoners" approach to anyone who dared to question Rick Warren was a real contrast to his kinder, gentler predecessor. If Thurston and Abanes were to be believed, there were absolutely no New Age implications to anything Warren was saying or doing. While I will not attempt to reply to all of their arguments, I will address two of them in this chapter and then several others later in the book.

Regarding Bernie Siegel

The fact that Rick Warren cited Bernie Siegel to introduce his ideas on "hope" and "purpose" initially caught Warren's first apologist, Gilbert Thurston, off guard. After discovering that Siegel was a key New Age leader, Thurston admitted the following in his report:

> To be honest with you, I was unaware of this source's background until Mr. Smith pointed it out in his book.[8]

But then Thurston tried to deflect the New Age implications by attempting to minimize what Rick Warren had done. He wrote:

> This is a fine line to walk. The question here is whether or not you the reader, Rick Warren, Mr. Smith and myself have ever been influenced or taught something by an unbeliever at anytime in our lives? The answer . . . of course.[9]

He went on to rationalize that "real truth is truth" even if it comes from someone who has a spirit-guide named "George." Thurston said:

> Knowing now that Bernie Siegel is a New Ager didn't make this statement any less of truth than if I had found out he was the world's best Christian doctor. Real truth is truth as long as it's biblical, no matter what the source.[10]

His statement "real truth is truth" would be the same argument that his successor Richard Abanes would make as Abanes also tried to downplay the New Age implications of the Bernie Siegel matter. Abanes wrote:

> Rick Warren feels, as I do, that a person does not have to be a Christian in order to make an astute observation, or say something that is true. All "truth" (wherever it may be found) is God's truth. For example, a true observation about the way people think or feel is a true observation—no matter who says it. So if I quote something that is true in order to make a point, then it really doesn't matter who said it, whether they were a Buddhist, an atheist, or a space alien![11]

However, author Tamara Hartzell notes that Richard Abanes was using the same argument New Age occultist Alice Bailey made regarding the validity of truth being truth "wherever it may be found." In her excellent book on Rick Warren titled *In the Name of Purpose: Sacrificing Truth on the Altar of Unity*, Hartzell cites the Bailey quote that is so similar to Abanes:

> "Another point which should be remembered is that in the new generation lies hope . . . because of the promptness with which *they recognize truth wherever it is to be found.*"[12]

The "all truth is God's truth" defense of Rick Warren's reference to Bernie Siegel reflects a real lack of concern for readers who might take Warren's positive reference to Siegel as an endorsement of Siegel himself. Curious readers might proceed to track down Siegel's New Age books where they will then learn how to meditate, contact personal spirit guides, and generally involve themselves in New Age teachings. The issue is not "all truth is God's truth," but why, under any circumstance, would Warren reference an occult/New Age author who could potentially stumble someone? Speaking to this same issue but in a different context, the apostle Paul warns believers not to do anything that might stumble someone: "But take heed lest by any means this liberty of yours become a stumblingblock to them that are weak" (1 Corinthians 8:9).

This seemingly generous but ill-conceived teaching that "all truth is God's truth" is also popular with many in today's alternative *emerging church* movement. But just because something contains some elements of truth, it doesn't mean that it is "God's truth" or that it is appropriate to reference that information. John 17:17 states: "Sanctify them through thy truth: thy word is truth." It is God's Word that is "God's truth"—not some statement that Bernie Siegel or someone else makes. Former Moody Memorial Church Pastor Dr. Harry Ironside (1876-1951) warned about the danger of this deceptive notion that "all truth is God's truth," when he wrote:

> Error is like leaven, of which we read, "A little leaven leaveneth the whole lump." Truth mixed with error is equivalent to all error, except that it is more innocent looking and, therefore, more dangerous. God hates such a mixture! Any error, or any truth-and-error mixture, calls for definite exposure and repudiation. To condone such is to be unfaithful to God and His Word and treacherous to imperiled souls for whom Christ died.[13]

Our spiritual adversary Satan—"the god of this world" (2

Corinthians 4:4)—inspires people to repeat pithy maxims like "all truth is God's truth" so he can slip a false teacher like Bernie Siegel into a highly popular book like *The Purpose Driven Life* that will sell over thirty million copies and be read by nearly fifty million people.[14] It is one thing to appropriately cite an occasional unbeliever, but Bernie Siegel isn't just *any* unbeliever. He is a key New Age leader with ties to both the occult and to Robert Schuller.[15] Schuller used Bernie Siegel to make a point about "hope" and "purpose" more than a decade before Rick Warren used Siegel to make his point about "hope" and "purpose."[16]

"All truth is God's truth" does not even come close to answering the legitimate question of why a Christian leader would cite a New Age proponent rather than Jesus Christ to introduce his ideas on "hope" and "purpose." The Bible makes it clear that when it comes to "hope," Jesus Christ is our only true "hope" in this world (1 Timothy 1:1).

Regarding Robert Schuller

It soon became evident to me that the intent of Saddleback apologists was to refute any of the New Age implications I had raised concerning Rick Warren. However, they made several key admissions regarding Robert Schuller and the obvious influence he had on Warren. In his Saddleback report, Gilbert Thurston stated:

> It is Mr. Smith's conclusion as well as our own that Robert Schuller has gotten off the track of traditional Christianity. However we also believe that Rick Warren has been able to successfully separate the wheat from the chaff of his learnings from Schuller.[17]

While Thurston agreed that Rick Warren had been influenced by Schuller's books and teachings over the years, he also tried to claim that Warren had eventually "separated himself theologically" from Schuller. Thurston wrote:

There is no question that Robert Schuller has been an influence on Rick through the years. As Mr. Smith points out, certain words, phrases and other teaching tools continue to show up, even to this day, in Rick's writings and teaching that he learned from the books of Robert Schuller.

However, this is where the similarities and influence end. Through the years as Robert Schuller's teachings have become more liberal and universalistic, Rick has separated himself theologically from Robert Schuller.[18]

But Saddleback apologists would avoid the fact that Rick Warren's use of Schuller terms went well beyond the claim that Warren only used them as catchy "phrases" or as "teaching tools." These seemingly innocent Schuller phrases are often loaded with spiritual meaning that have serious New Age implications. Schuller terms like "God's Dream" and "New Reformation" are found to be at the heart of Warren's present-day Purpose Driven movement.

The Saddleback report sent out to inquiring pastors regarding Robert Schuller's influence in Rick Warren's ministry does not tell the whole story. Anyone with discernment watching Schuller over the years is aware that Schuller's teachings haven't *become* more "liberal and universalistic"—they have *always* been "liberal and universalistic"! It is not that he has *gotten* "off the track of traditional Christianity"—he has *always* been "off the track of traditional Christianity." For years, people have been warned about Schuller's errant teachings and New Age sympathies. Dave Hunt and T.A. McMahon's best-selling 1985 book, *The Seduction of Christianity: Spiritual Discernment in the Last Days* has a strong warning to everyone to stay away from Schuller's hybridized New Age "Christianity." In *The Seduction of Christianity*, Hunt and Mc-Mahon describe a visit Schuller made many years ago to the New

Age Unity School of Christianity headquarters near Kansas City, Missouri. During his talk, Schuller was asked about the New Age:

> "Dr. Schuller," he was asked, "we hear a lot of talk these days about the New Age, the Age of Aquarius, the type of New Age thinking that we are involved in with Holistic healing and various other things that are part of what is called the New Age. Will you describe the role of what you might consider the New Age minister in the '80s and beyond?" Schuller made no protest that he knew nothing of the New Age or that he wasn't a "New Age minister." Without hesitating, he replied:

> "Well, I think it depends upon where you're working. I believe that the responsibility in this Age is to 'positivize' religion. Now this probably doesn't have much bearing to you people, being Unity people, you're positive. But I talk a great deal to groups that are not positive . . . even to what we would call Fundamentalists who deal constantly with words like sin, salvation, repentance, guilt, that sort of thing.

> "So when I'm dealing with these people . . . what we have to do is positivize the words that have classically only had a negative interpretation."[19]

Yet for whatever reason, countless numbers of pastors have chosen to disregard the many warnings about Robert Schuller's unbiblical teachings and New Age affections. I couldn't help but wonder if having a large successful church like Schuller's was more important to these pastors than heeding the warnings to stay away from false teachings. Schuller's well-known spiritual ties to his long-time "mentor,"[20] the late Norman Vincent Peale, should have been enough to alert anyone to keep their distance from Schuller.

Three

The New Age Peale Factor

Whatever may be the embarrassment caused by these striking similarities [between Norman Vincent Peale and New Age author Florence Scovel Shinn], it pales against the discomfiture that millions of mainline Christians, purporting to stand on orthodoxy and Scripture alone, have thus unwittingly embraced the Occult. So strong is its tacit foothold that it now may well be the primary working faith of many in the churches.[1]

—*Lutheran Quarterly*, **Summer 1995**

In March 2005, I received a letter and two accompanying articles from an Indiana pastor. One of the articles was clipped from the August 3, 1995 *Indianapolis Star* newspaper. It featured a big picture of Norman Vincent Peale with a headline and subtitle that read:

> Norman Vincent Peale accused of plagiarism: 'Power of Positive Thinking' author's work similar to that of a little-known teacher of occult science.[2]

The *Indianapolis Star* article asked the question: "Was the Rev. Norman Vincent Peale, father of the 'believe and succeed' theology sweeping American Protestantism, a plagiarist inspired by the occult?" In attempting to answer this question, the newspaper referred to an article from a *Lutheran Quarterly* journal that contended that Peale drew much of his inspiration from the writings and teachings of occult/New Age author Florence Scovel Shinn.

Presenting information from the *Lutheran Quarterly* article, the *Indianapolis Star* reported:

> After comparing his book to hers, the authors cite scores of specific instances in which Peale and Shinn not only think alike, but use similar or identical phrases. . . .
>
> Shinn, who died in 1940, drew on mystical sources dating to the ancient Egyptian philosopher Hermes Trismegistus ["as above, so below"] and the secrets of Freemasonry.
>
> Such sources are progenitors of New Age, a movement considered ungodly hocus-pocus by conservative and fundamentalist Christians. . . .
>
> Shinn's privately published metaphysical works, reissued by both Simon & Schuster and the Church of Religious Science, are available in New Age bookstores. Peale penned the introduction to the Simon & Schuster edition, indicating he had "long used" Shinn's teachings.[3]

The *Lutheran Quarterly* article that the *Indianapolis Star* had referenced regarding Peale's unattributed use of Shinn's occult/New Age teachings, with Peale/Shinn side-by-side quotes, clearly demonstrated the likeness of their writings. The *Lutheran Quarterly* article stated:

> The striking similarity between these passages discloses an unsettling theological secret. Along with many other parallel concepts, affirmations, metaphors, and stories, they provide testimony that the writing that made Norman Vincent Peale "minister to millions" and a millionaire many times over, shows a startling similarity to the writings of an obscure teacher

of Occult science named Florence Scovel Shinn. Whatever may be the embarrassment caused by these striking similarities, it pales against the discomfiture that millions of mainline Christians, purporting to stand on orthodoxy and Scripture alone, have thus unwittingly embraced the Occult. So strong is its tacit foothold that it now may well be the primary working faith of many in the churches.[4]

In the 1986 reissue of Shinn's 1925 book, *The Game of Life and How to Play It*, Norman Vincent Peale's front and back cover endorsements of her occult/New Age book respectively read:

> *The Game of Life* is filled with wisdom and creative insights. That its teachings will work I know to be fact, for I've long used them myself.

> By studying and practicing the principles laid down in this book one may find prosperity, solve problems, have better health, achieve good personal relations— in a word, win the game of life.[5]

Peale's New Age Endorsements

In his letter to me, the Indiana pastor wrote how he remembered the *Lutheran Quarterly* article after reading my book *Deceived on Purpose*. My observation that Rick Warren emulated so many of Robert Schuller's ideologies reminded him of Norman Vincent Peale's alleged unattributed use of Florence Scovel Shinn's writings. The Indiana pastor was surprised I had not mentioned the New Age link between Peale and Schuller. He said that the New Age implications of Warren's teachings did not stop with Schuller or even with Schuller's mentor, Peale. It stretched back through all of them to the occult itself.

With this new information concerning Norman Vincent Peale, I looked a little more deeply into his background. I discovered that

Peale had been a 33rd degree Mason[6] and that he had endorsed other New Age books through the years. One of these books was written by Bernie Siegel—the man Robert Schuller and Rick Warren had both positively referenced in regard to "hope" and "purpose." Although I had been aware of the Schuller/Warren link to Siegel, I had not been aware of the Peale link. The Bernie Siegel book that Peale endorsed was *Love, Medicine & Miracles*—the book where Siegel described how he contacted his personal spirit guide "George" in a guided meditation. Peale's endorsement on the back cover read:

> In these pages is found a precious secret, that of health and well-being.[7]

Siegel's continued New Age activity includes his teaching in New Age leader Neale Donald Walsch's School of the New Spirituality.[8] As previously mentioned, Walsch has described Robert Schuller as an "extraordinary minister"—someone who could spark a "New Reformation" that could help bring the world together as "One." Walsch also praised the "extraordinary insight" of Norman Vincent Peale in Walsch's 2005 book, *What God Wants*. In discussing oc-cult/New Age manifestation (how individuals attempt to use their feelings and imagination to create events outside themselves), Walsch commends Peale and two New Age authors, Esther and Jerry Hicks. It is Esther Hicks and a group of spirit guides named "Abraham" that helped inspire Rhonda Byrne's Oprah Winfrey endorsed, best-selling 2006 book *The Secret*.[9] In *What God Wants*, Walsch writes the following about Peale:

> This phenomenon [occult manifestation] is discussed with extraordinary insight in the classic book *The Power of Positive Thinking*, written over fifty years ago by the Reverend Dr. Norman Vincent Peale, a Christian minister who understood that feelings are a gift from God, giving us the power of creation. That book has sold millions of copies and

is still easy to find today, in libraries, in bookstores, and from any online bookseller.

A more updated and non-Christian-oriented look at this amazing process is offered in the contemporary book *Ask and It Is Given*, by Esther and Jerry Hicks....

The fact that you can create something by picturing it in your mind, by *seeing it* as already accomplished, and by allowing yourself to experience the *feeling* associated with that is evidence of the greatest news humanity has ever heard.[10]

This creative visualization technique that Neale Donald Walsch is commending is at the heart of the New Age movement's attempt to create a "positive future" by universally affirming and envisioning that we are all "One" because God is "in" everyone and everything. This attempt by the New Age to create a positive future by affirming "oneness" is deceptively appealing but very unbiblical. The Bible states that we are only "one" through our personal commitment to Jesus Christ as our Lord and Savior (Romans 3:23-25; Galatians 3:26-28). The Bible makes it clear that God is not "in" everyone and everything (Ezekiel 28:2; Hosea 11:9; John 2:24-25; Romans 1:21-23).

I discovered that another occult/New Age book Norman Vincent Peale had endorsed was Ernest Holmes' *The Science of Mind*. In *Deceived on Purpose*, I recounted an incident that a minister of Religious Science shared with me.[11] She said that she and her husband—both New Age ministers—had attended Robert Schuller's Institute for Successful Church Leadership in the early 1970s. When she talked to Schuller in his office and explained that she was a Religious Science minister, Schuller pulled Ernest Holmes' book *The Science of Mind* from his bottom desk drawer as an obvious gesture of fellowship. The late Holmes (1887-1960) was the founder of the Church of Religious Science and his book *The Science of Mind* is regarded by many in the occult as a New Age "bible."

Echoing the foundational teaching of the New Age/New World Religion that God is "in" everyone, Peale applauded Holmes saying, "I believe God was in this man, Ernest Holmes. He was in tune with the infinite."[12]

I also discovered that Peale had endorsed Unity minister Eric Butterworth's book *Discover the Power Within You*. This occult/New Age book has nearly one hundred references to the "Divinity of Man" and was cited by Oprah Winfrey in 1987 and again in 2008, as the book that changed her Christian worldview to a New Age worldview. In a 1987 Oprah Winfrey Show titled "The New Age Movement," Oprah said:

> One of the most important books, I think I've read in my life was a book by Eric Butterworth. . . . called *Discover the Power Within You*. And what Eric Butterworth said in that book is that Jesus did not come to teach how divine he was, but came to teach us that there is divinity within us.[13]

Norman Vincent Peale's endorsement on the back cover of Butterworth's book leaves no question as to his spiritual propensities:

> A wonderful book . . . truly a life-changer, as many readers know. This book really does release the power within us all.[14]

Yet another New Age book Peale endorsed and wrote the foreword to is the late John Marks Templeton's book *Discovering the Laws of Life*. Templeton was a wealthy business leader, philanthropist, and New Age sympathizer that Robert Schuller interviewed and put on the cover of his 1986 *Possibilities* magazine.[15] In *Deceived on Purpose*, I describe how Rick Warren was one of the judges for Templeton's 2004 Power of Purpose Essay Contest. Just as Bernie Siegel had a connection with Robert Schuller, Rick Warren, and Norman Vincent Peale, so New Age proponent John Marks Templeton had a connection with these same three men.

As Above, So Below and the Saddleback Apologists

The information sent to me by the Indiana pastor about Norman Vincent Peale is astounding. It reveals that Florence Scovel Shinn—the occult author Peale had endorsed and was accused of plagiarizing—had drawn upon the ancient teachings of Hermes Trismegistus. As previously cited, Hermes Trismegistus is said to be the author of the ancient, mystical saying "as above, so below" that signifies God is "in" everything. The *Indianapolis Star* newspaper article sent to me stated:

> Shinn, who died in 1940, drew on mystical sources dating to the ancient Egyptian philosopher Hermes Trismegistus and the secrets of Freemasonry.
>
> Such sources are progenitors of New Age.[16]

In their attempt to nullify the New Age implications of Eugene Peterson's *The Message* and Rick Warren's predominant use of this "paraphrase," Saddleback apologists expressed no concern about Peterson's insertion of the occult phrase "as above, so below" into the middle of the Lord's Prayer. In their rush to defend Warren's use of *The Message* paraphrase, they tried to make me the issue rather than the occult/New Age phrase.

Saddleback apologists may have hoped the whole issue of "as above, so below" would quietly go away—but it did not. The term "as above, so below," with its mystical God "in" everything meaning, was prominently featured on the front page of author Rhonda Byrne's best-selling book, *The Secret*. As already mentioned, *The Secret* was largely inspired by the teachings of a group of spirit guides named "Abraham" channeled by New Age medium Esther Hicks—the same Esther Hicks that Neale Donald Walsch had praised (along with Peale) in regard to occult manifestation. Hicks had simply updated Peale's teachings on how to create your own reality through the practice of occult/New Age techniques—the same techniques Peale had gleaned from Florence Scovel Shinn and other New Age teachers.

The main "secret" of *The Secret* was contained in the book's full front-page display of the phrase "as above, so below"—God "in" everything. The New Age/New Spirituality "secret" is that we are all God because God is "in" everyone and everything—the foundational teaching of the proposed coming New World Religion. This Hermes Trismegistus "as above, so below" secret was revealed and underscored by author Rhonda Byrne when she wrote in her book: "You are God in a physical body."[17]

Peale—"God is in you"

In his famous 1952 book *The Power of Positive Thinking*, Norman Vincent Peale presented the foundational teaching of the coming New World Religion—the as above, so below teaching that God is "in" everyone. Peale told the millions of readers of that book: "God is in you."[18] Fifty years later, Robert Schuller echoed his mentor's words when he told his worldwide television audience the very same thing—"Yes, God is alive and He is in every single human being!"[19] Rick Warren similarly tells readers of *The Purpose Driven Life* that the Bible says God "is in everything."[20]

I found it remarkable that the pastor from Indiana had encouraged me to look more fully at the occult roots of Norman Vincent Peale's ministry and to see the New Age implications this had for both Robert Schuller and Rick Warren. Given Peale's influence on Schuller and Schuller's influence on Warren, the last thing Warren needed was for someone to bring Norman Vincent Peale's obvious occultism into the light.

Four

George Mair's Book

But in the 1990s, following in the footsteps of Peale and Schuller, the leader of the next generation of Church Growth Movement pastors emerged. That man was none other than Rick Warren.[1]

     —George Mair, *A Life With Purpose*

In April 2005, a new book was published about Rick Warren. It was titled *A Life With Purpose: Reverend Rick Warren: The Most Inspiring Pastor of Our Time.* The book was an extremely favorable presentation of Warren and the Purpose Driven movement. Author George Mair genuinely liked and respected Warren as he described the Saddleback pastor's life and ministry. Mair's book was carried in major bookstores around the country—including Christian bookstores. The author's high regard for Warren was evident throughout *A Life With Purpose.* Early on in his book, Mair writes:

> I knew one thing for sure about Rick Warren: his is a fascinating story. A humble man with humble beginnings, he is changing America—and the world—"one soul at a time."[2]
>
> After hearing him preach and experiencing Saddleback Church, I understand why millions are listening to this man, and knew that the story

behind the movement deserves to be told.[3]

> His demeanor as the founder and pastor of one of
> the largest churches in the world reflects a man whose
> focus is on his mission to serve the Lord by bringing
> in the unchurched souls—the lost sheep—to embrace
> and celebrate the saving Grace of Jesus Christ.[4]

A *Life With Purpose* is filled with continuous praise for Rick
Warren and his Purpose Driven ministry. Nothing George Mair
said could be considered negative or critical about Warren. In
fact, the rare comment of a critic is usually offset by the author
himself. For example, Mair states:

> Another thing those critics fail to take into account
> is the role that Rick himself plays in the phenomenal
> growth of his church. Rick Warren is a truly
> charismatic spiritual leader. It's clear to anyone who
> experiences one of his Saddleback services that he
> truly loves what he does. He relishes standing up at
> the podium, looking out at the smiling crowd, and
> sharing the Good News of Jesus.[5]

"New Age Preacher" Norman Vincent Peale

There is no question that A *Life With Purpose* is an overwhelmingly positive account of Rick Warren and the Purpose Driven
movement. However, at one point George Mair—in an almost
naive and non-judgmental way—talks about Norman Vincent
Peale and the New Age influence Peale had exerted on the
Church Growth movement. Mair frames his remarks about Peale
by writing:

> The numbers speak for themselves. The Church
> Growth Movement has been wildly successful in
> Southern California . . . as well as in the rest of the

country. Which prompts us to ask: what are the roots of this powerful movement? Rick Warren may be the foremost figure in the CGM today, but he's only a piece—albeit an important one—of a greater development in the Christian Church. Who and what gave birth to this movement in which Rick would play such a vital role?[6]

Mair answers his own question by stating what other writers have known and also set forth—that it was Norman Vincent Peale who really provided the spiritual foundation of today's Church Growth movement. In a sub-section titled "Laying the Groundwork: New Age Preacher Norman Vincent Peale," Mair writes:

> Reverend Norman Vincent Peale is, to many, the most prophetic and moving New Age preacher of the twentieth century. He is also the father of the self-help movement that formed the groundwork for the Church Growth Movement. Peale formed perhaps the most dramatic and meaningful link between religion and psychology of any religious leader in history. It is this same approachable, therapeutic brand of religion that many mega churches, including Saddleback, put forward today. It is this kind of religion that is so appealing to the masses of unchurched men and women that Rick Warren hopes to reach.[7]

George Mair goes on to state that Saddleback Church "distinctly bears the stamp of Norman Vincent Peale":

> Peale's ministry was the first to raise the question that still faces mega churches today: is it spiritual compromise if a pastor simplifies his message in order to make it appealing to a huge number of seekers?[8]

His biographer, [Carol R.] George, says, "Norman

Vincent Peale is undoubtedly one of the most
controversial figures in modern American
Christianity." But no matter what people think
about his theories, they have to acknowledge Peale's
remarkable unification of psychology and theology.
Without that unification, mega churches wouldn't
exist today. . . . In that sense, Saddleback distinctly
bears the stamp of Reverend Norman Vincent Peale.[9]

While Mair explains that it was Peale who laid the New Age
"groundwork" for today's Church Growth movement, he notes
that it was Robert Schuller who helped to create the effectiveness
of the megachurch movement on a national scale:

But it's hard to argue that Schuller was not the first
person to be *effective* on a national scale. He was
unquestionably a pioneer in the Church Growth
Movement and a major influence on Rick Warren.[10]

In his book, George Mair notes that Rick Warren had attended the Robert H. Schuller Institute for Successful Church
Leadership.[11] Then, after describing some of the various church
growth leaders up to and including the 1980s, Mair writes:

But in the 1990s, following in the footsteps of Peale
and Schuller, the leader of the next generation of
Church Growth Movement pastors emerged. That
man was none other than Rick Warren.[12]

Occult/New Age Influence: Peale to Schuller to Warren

In researching his book, George Mair had discovered the same
Lutheran Quarterly article sent to me the month before by the
Indiana pastor. Citing the article, Mair wrote how Norman
Vincent Peale had been accused of plagiarizing material from an
occult source:

Some of Peale's former colleagues and another minister went so far as to accuse him of plagiarism. Writing in the *Lutheran Quarterly*, Reverend John Gregory Tweed of Fort Lauderdale, Florida, and Reverend George D. Exoo of Pittsburgh wrote that many of Peale's uplifting affirmations originated with an "obscure teacher of occult science" named Florence Scovel Shinn. They based this charge on their comparison of words in Peale's writings and those of Shinn's book, *The Game of Life and How to Play It*, in which they found some identical phrases.[13]

In *A Life With Purpose*, George Mair also reveals that Norman Vincent Peale had been accused of using unattributed material from occult/New Age author Florence Scovel Shinn. From my own research that had been spurred by that same *Lutheran Quarterly* article, I learned that Peale had much more interest and involvement in the occult than I realized. He had openly endorsed the works of key New Age figures like Ernest Holmes, Eric Butterworth, and Bernie Siegel. Because questions had already arisen regarding Rick Warren's undiscerning reference to Siegel and Warren's use of unaccredited material from Robert Schuller in the *The Purpose Driven Life*, the very last thing Warren needed was a book—no matter how much it praised him—intimating a New Age link running from Peale to Schuller to Warren himself. In short, Warren did not need any more New Age implications arising that would cast further doubt upon his Purpose Driven movement. But ironically—at least on the surface—it wasn't Mair's remarks about Peale that stirred up concern at Saddleback Church but rather an offhand remark Mair had made in his book about author and businessman Ken Blanchard.

Ken Blanchard and Rick Warren

In *A Life With Purpose*, George Mair states that Rick Warren had "hired" business leader Ken Blanchard to train and equip church leaders in conjunction with Warren's P.E.A.C.E. Plan. Again, with nothing but praise for Warren and Blanchard, Mair writes:

> Rick Warren says that we need leaders—but what kind? Do we need more of Bill Gates, Jack Welch, and Warren Buffett? Rick says no. Not when we already have a perfect leader in Jesus Christ. We need to learn to lead like Jesus.
>
> Here, as he always does, Rick taps the best and the most famous to help train church leaders to be like Jesus. He has hired Ken Blanchard, author of best-selling *The One Minute Manager*, to come to Saddleback to help train people how to be effective leaders at home, in business, in school, and in church. It is a dramatic and impressive move, one that is typical of Rick Warren.[14]

As noted in *Deceived on Purpose*, Rick Warren first described his 5-step Global P.E.A.C.E. Plan on November 2, 2003. In introducing the P.E.A.C.E. Plan to his congregation and to those watching on the Internet, Warren mentioned the names of two key people in regard to his P.E.A.C.E. Plan—authors Bruce Wilkinson and Ken Blanchard. *Prayer of Jabez* author Wilkinson had just released a book titled *The Dream Giver* that was being promoted in conjunction with the P.E.A.C.E. Plan. Wilkinson had been at Saddleback the previous week to support the Schulleresque "God's Dream" theme Warren was using to underscore his P.E.A.C.E. Plan. The other person Warren was bringing into the picture was Ken Blanchard, co-founder of the newly formed Lead Like Jesus organization.

In introducing the leadership part of his P.E.A.C.E. Plan, Rick Warren described how the first "E" in his P.E.A.C.E. Plan stood for "equip leaders." He informed his congregation that Ken Blanchard had "signed on" to help train leaders "around the world." Warren stated:

> That's why, on November 20, on a Thursday in a couple of weeks, Ken Blanchard and I are going to teach a national, nationwide simulcast called "Learning to Lead Like Jesus." And we'll be broadcasting it from Birmingham, but this is one of the churches we're going to do it in, obviously, our own church. And so we'll be coming here and I'm hoping you'll be able to take the day off and come for a full day of leadership training. Now, if you don't know who Ken Blanchard is, he wrote the best-selling leadership book of all time . . . *One Minute Manager* and a dozen other best sellers. But when he became a Christian, he said, "You know, Rick, I'm becoming less and less enamored with the American style of leadership and the American business modules of leadership which tend to be pretty manipulative. And I am more and more impressed with Jesus who was the perfect leader." And so we need to learn to lead like Jesus.
>
> Now Ken has signed on to help with the P.E.A.C.E. Plan. And he's going to be helping train us in leadership and in how to train others to be leaders all around the world.[15]

From all appearances, Ken Blanchard would be playing an important role in helping to fulfill the "equip leaders" part of Rick Warren's Global P.E.A.C.E. Plan. This was confirmed two weeks later when Warren appeared with Blanchard at the Lead Like Jesus Celebration in Birmingham. When Warren spoke at the conference, he stated that he and Blanchard were "working together" on the P.E.A.C.E. Plan:

> [T]here is a dramatic shortage of servant leadership
> in the world. I've traveled all around the world, and
> people are following the wrong model of leadership. . . .
> So, we've come up with a little plan called the peace plan.
> You and I [addressing Blanchard] are working together
> on this. The peace plan, P E A C E, Jesus, the master
> servant leader, was the Prince of Peace. . . . P stands
> for plant churches, E stands for equip leaders, and
> that's what we're here for today. . . . It is my goal and
> vision and your goal and vision to be used of God
> to raise up millions and millions of local churches
> and businesses and everybody else to plant churches,
> equip leaders, assist the poor, care for the sick, and
> educate the next generation. That can only be done
> when we get the right model of leadership.[16]

After Warren's remarks about what he and Ken Blanchard
hoped to accomplish together, Blanchard shared what Warren had
said to him just before they went up to speak. Warren told him,
"You know, Ken, let's start a revolution."[17] Then Blanchard, with
Warren sitting right next to him, proceeded to tell the audience
how Norman Vincent Peale had been instrumental in helping
him to come to the Lord fifteen years previous. Blanchard stated:

> And God started sending me this team, Bob Buford,
> Norman Vincent Peale, and [Bill] Hybels. All kinds
> of people started coming after me. I finally joined
> up in 1987-88 and turned my life over to the Lord.[18]

Lighthouse Trails Press Release

It was not until the release of George Mair's book in 2005 that
some people learned that Rick Warren had announced back in
2003 that Ken Blanchard would be working with him on the
P.E.A.C.E. Plan. When Lighthouse Trails Publishing learned
about Blanchard's involvement with Warren, they were con-

cerned. One of their authors, Ray Yungen, had been researching the New Age for many years and often came across Blanchard, who had been consistently endorsing and writing the forewords to New Age books and organizations. On April 19, 2005, Lighthouse Trails issued a press release, quoting George Mair's book that Warren had "hired" Blanchard to work with him on the P.E.A.C.E. Plan.[19] Lighthouse Trails warned of the serious New Age implications of allowing someone as undiscerning as Blanchard to teach Christians around the world how to "lead like Jesus." The press release documented many of Blanchard's New Age endorsements including Deepak Chopra's book, *The Seven Spiritual Laws of Success* and a book titled *What Would Buddha Do at Work?* for which Blanchard wrote the foreword.

Another book that Ken Blanchard endorsed is *Little Wave and Old Swell,* written by Blanchard's longtime friend and business associate, Jim Ballard—an avid devotee of the late Hindu guru Paramahansa Yogananda. In fact, Blanchard wrote the forewords to both the 2004 and 2007 editions of *Little Wave and Old Swell.* He states that *Little Wave and Old Swell* is a book for "people of all faiths." In the foreword of the 2004 edition, Blanchard writes:

> Love is love. For that reason this little volume should not be thought of as a "religious" book. It is one of those rare stories whose message transcends ideas that divide people. It is for people of all faiths, as well as for those of no faith . . . .
>
> *Little Wave and Old Swell* is a book for the innocent seeker, young or old, in each one of us. It's a book to read alone and contemplate.[20]

But the "message" this Blanchard-endorsed book has for the "innocent seeker" is the foundational teaching of the New Age/New Spirituality—we are all "one" because God is "in" everyone and everything. In the 2007 edition (also with a foreword by Blanchard), Jim Ballard writes:

[Old Swell] read Little Wave's mind. "You are a moving wrinkle on the seamless fabric of the Great Deep," he said. "You thought that you were separate, but no. You can never be apart from your Source.

"Know now that you and I and all our brother and sister waves are One with the Great Deep.

"We have always been One.
We shall always be One."[21]

At the very end of the story, the author offers a New Age prayer: "Help me to feel the Oneness within all things."[22]

Lead Like Which Jesus?

On the day Rick Warren introduced his P.E.A.C.E. Plan at Saddleback Church and announced that Ken Blanchard had "signed on" to help with the P.E.A.C.E. Plan, George Mair was sitting in the congregation. At the time, Mair probably had no idea that Blanchard had endorsed New Age books and had personal ties to Norman Vincent Peale. He had assumed that when someone "signed on" they had been "hired"—an understandable assumption. But Warren and Saddleback apologist Richard Abanes were quick to take Mair to task for saying Blanchard had been "hired" by Warren. They said Blanchard had not been "hired." He had volunteered. This issue would become a major point of contention for Warren and his Saddleback defense team. In using it, attention would be deflected away from the real problem of Blanchard's New Age sympathies and Warren's wanting to utilize him to train leaders worldwide for the P.E.A.C.E. Plan.

Suddenly George Mair was a target for stating that Rick Warren had "hired" Ken Blanchard to train people around the world to "lead like Jesus." It was not George Mair, but the Lighthouse Trails press release that brought Blanchard's New Age propensities to light. Yet despite Saddleback's effort to discredit George Mair and his book, the question many people were asking was—"why would a self-professing Evangelical Christian like Rick Warren choose a New Age sympathizer like Ken Blanchard to train people to 'lead like Jesus?'" And just what "Jesus" was Blanchard pointing people to—the Jesus of the Bible or the "Jesus" of the New Age? Did Blanchard even know the difference? Obviously, the "Jesus" of the New Age/New Spirituality books that Blanchard has often endorsed is "another Jesus." In fact, the apostle Paul chides the Ken Blanchards of his day for their lack of spiritual discernment and their willingness to "bear with" and even follow "another Jesus," who is not the real Jesus Christ (2 Corinthians 11:4). Paul's words also pertain to Rick Warren for his willingness to use someone as undiscerning and spiritually misled as Blanchard:

> For if he that cometh preacheth another Jesus, whom we have not preached, or if ye receive another spirit, which ye have not received, or another gospel, which ye have not accepted, ye might well bear with him.

In Matthew 24:3-5 the real Jesus Christ warns about false Christs—like the New Age Christ—who would come in His name at the end of time to deceive even the elect, if that were possible. With all of this information about Blanchard coming to the surface, the big question was how would Rick Warren deal with Blanchard's New Age entanglements?

Five

Blaming the Messenger

THERE IS ALMOST NOTHING CORRECT IN
MAIR'S BOOK.[1]

—e-mail from Rick Warren to Lighthouse Trails

In a May 31, 2005 midnight e-mail to Lighthouse Trails Publishing, Rick Warren made it clear that he was not happy with George Mair *or* with Lighthouse Trails regarding the subject of Ken Blanchard. With an apparent effort to take the spotlight off Blanchard's New Age affinities, Warren attempted to place it on George Mair and Lighthouse Trails instead.

With no documentation, Rick Warren immediately accused Mair of having "literally hundreds of errors and made-up conclusions" in *A Life with Purpose*. At the same time, he took Lighthouse Trails to task for relying on anything that Mair wrote in his book. Ironically, the only thing that Lighthouse Trails had quoted from *A Life with Purpose* was the statement that Warren had "hired" Ken Blanchard to help with his P.E.A.C.E. Plan. The April 19, 2005 Lighthouse Trails Press release stated:

> According to a new biography on Rick Warren, *A Life With Purpose* written by George Mair, Rick Warren has solicited the services of Ken Blanchard to aid

him in training leaders: "Rick taps the best and most
famous to help train church leaders to be like Jesus. He
has hired Ken Blanchard . . . . to come to Saddleback to
help train people how to be effective leaders."[2]

Rick Warren didn't seem to understand how a reasonable
person could misinterpret the phrase "signed on" to mean
"hired." True, George Mair had assumed that "signed on" meant
"hired," but that was not even the issue Lighthouse Trails was
raising. The issue was why would Warren choose a New Age
sympathizer like Ken Blanchard to "equip" leaders around the
world to "lead like Jesus"? Lighthouse Trails was not focusing on
George Mair's book—only on Blanchard's New Age sympathies.
Mair just happened to be the one who mentioned that Warren
would be working with Blanchard to equip leaders. What proved
to be so revealing to those watching Rick Warren, was how he
and his apologists turned the tables on people. Rather than
dealing with the New Age implications of the Purpose Driven
movement, they tried to discredit those of us they perceived to
be "critics." In this case, George Mair and Lighthouse Trails became the "problem" rather than Blanchard's New Age affections.

Rick Warren's midnight e-mail to Lighthouse Trails cited
his many unsubstantiated objections to George Mair's book.
Interestingly, that e-mail was posted on the Internet by Richard
Abanes within just a few hours after Warren sent it to Lighthouse Trails.[3] It began circulating quickly, and within twenty-
four hours, Lighthouse Trails was receiving calls and e-mails
about Warren's e-mail to them. Lighthouse Trails would later
post a point-by-point response to Warren's e-mail, contending
that most—if not all—of his complaints regarding George Mair's
book and the Lighthouse Trails Press Release were generally
misstated and simply not true. Warren's e-mail and the Lighthouse Trails point-by-point refutation are still posted at www.
lighthousetrailsresearch.com.

Thou Dost Protest Too Much

In his e-mail to Lighthouse Trails, the pastor with a reputation for being "seeker-friendly" was anything but "seeker-friendly" with George Mair. Although Rick Warren has stated on numerous occasions that there are 2.3 billion Christians* in the world, he made it clear in his e-mail he did not consider Mair to be one of them. Even though Mair described himself as a Christian (and actually was attending Saddleback for two years while he was writing *A Life with Purpose*), Warren dismissed Mair as "an unbeliever"—someone who "was not even born again." In questioning Mair's faith, Warren was trying to undermine Mair's credibility in commenting on anything pertaining to Warren and the Church Growth movement. In his e-mail to Lighthouse Trails, Warren wrote:

> George Mair, an unbeliever, evidently wanted to make a quick buck turning out a book on me, at the peak of the popularity of *The Purpose Driven Life* . . . Since he is not even born again, he certainly wouldn't understand theology, what I believe, or even the basics of our ministry.[4]

Perhaps hopeful that Mair's reference to "New Age prophet Norman Vincent Peale" would be buried along with the Lighthouse Trails documentation of Ken Blanchard's New Age endorsements, Warren made it seem that George Mair's book was completely worthless—even though Mair's book had nothing but effusive praise for Rick Warren and his ministry. Using capital letters to make his point and to express his displeasure with Mair, Warren wrote in the e-mail:

THERE IS ALMOST NOTHING CORRECT IN MAIR'S BOOK. Practically every page has either

---

* One instance when Warren gave this statistic was on August 17, 2006, when Rick Warren was interviewed by Charlie Rose. This may be viewed at http://video.google.com/videoplay?docid=-5555324196046364882.

a factual error, a made-up story, or Mair's weird interpretation of my motives and beliefs.[5]

After detailing these alleged "factual errors," Rick Warren added:

> I could go on and on, but any author who gets such basic facts wrong (that are easily checkable) should not be trusted with his interpretation of anything.[6]

In attempting to discredit George Mair, it appeared that Rick Warren was also attempting to discredit Lighthouse Trails and what they had written about Ken Blanchard. However, as Lighthouse Trails was quick to point out, it was Warren who was getting most of his facts wrong. For example, in regard to Blanchard's New Age endorsements, Warren stated in his e-mail to Lighthouse Trails that Blanchard's actions were the result of Blanchard being a "new believer." He said Blanchard should not be held responsible for those endorsements because they had been made before he was a Christian. He wrote:

> Ken is a new believer—a new creature in Christ. He should not be held accountable for statements or endorsements he made before he became a Christian. And he's just learning now.[7]

But Lighthouse Trails would show in their point-by-point refutation that Rick Warren's statement about Ken Blanchard being "a new believer" was not true—at least according to Blanchard, who, by his own description, had been a believer for fifteen years—since the late 1980s. In fact, Warren was sitting next to Blanchard at the 2003 Lead Like Jesus Celebration in Birmingham, Alabama when Blanchard described the date of his conversion to everyone at the conference. Blanchard told Warren and all those in attendance and watching on the simulcast that he had come to the Lord "in 1987-88." As previously mentioned, Blanchard stated:

> And God started sending me this team, Bob Buford,
> Norman Vincent Peale, and [Bill] Hybels. All kinds
> of people started coming after me. I finally joined
> up in 1987-88 and turned my life over to the Lord.[8]

Ken Blanchard, by his own description, was anything but "a new believer," contrary to what Rick Warren told Lighthouse Trails in the e-mail he made public through Richard Abanes. In addition to the Birmingham Lead Like Jesus Celebration, Blanchard described his 1987-88 conversion in his 1994 autobiography, *We are the Beloved: A Spiritual Journey.* In *We are the Beloved,* Blanchard similarly explained that prior to his conversion he had been spiritually prepared by Norman Vincent Peale, Bob Buford and Bill Hybels—three men associated with Robert Schuller.[9] The fact that Blanchard came to the Lord under the tutelage of Peale and two other colleagues of Schuller, explains a lot more about Blanchard's New Age endorsements than Warren's attempt to blame them on Blanchard being "a new believer."

Another New Age Link: Henri Nouwen

A website for Hindu Guru Paramahansa Yogananda discloses that *We Are the Beloved*—Blanchard's 1994 Christian testimony—is actually "ghost-written" by Blanchard's longtime New Age friend, associate, and Yogananda devotee Jim Ballard.[10] One of the people Blanchard dedicates his book to is Norman Vincent Peale.

Along with his praise of Norman Vincent Peale, Blanchard states that the title of his book—*We Are the Beloved*—was inspired by the late mystical/contemplative/Catholic priest Henri Nouwen's book, *Life of the Beloved.*[11] Blanchard quotes Nouwen frequently in his book and credits Leadership Network head, Bob Buford, for introducing him to the writings of Nouwen.[12] Many emergent and alternative church figures were trained by Bob Buford's Leadership Network. They too tout Nouwen and other mystics in their writings. Nouwen is a favorite of both Rick Warren and his wife, Kay. In Ray Yungen's book, *A Time of Departing,* which exposes the contemplative prayer movement, Yungen documents the Warrens' strong admiration for Nouwen as well as Warren's promotion of other contemplative prayer teachers.[13]

Interestingly, Robert Schuller incorporated Nouwen's ideas into the Institute for Successful Church Leadership that was attended by thousands of pastors, including Rick Warren. In addition, Schuller had Nouwen as a special guest on the *Hour of Power* television program in 1992. After Nouwen appeared on that program, his "reputation [among Protestants] blossomed dramatically."[14] In his book *Here and Now*, Henri Nouwen presents his bottom-line belief—that is also the bottom-line teaching of the New Age/New Spirituality—that God is "in" everyone. He wrote:

> The God who dwells in our inner sanctuary is also the God who dwells in the inner sanctuary of each human being.[15]

Nouwen's seductive but obviously false New Age teaching that God is "in" everyone parallels Robert Schuller's sermon at the Crystal Cathedral when he proclaimed that God is "in" every single human being.[16] This foundational teaching taught by Nouwen, Schuller and countless New Age teachers is, again, what Norman Vincent Peale taught in his 1952 book *The Power of Positive Thinking* when he wrote: "God is in you."[17]

Blanchard's Book with Peale

A probable key to Ken Blanchard's New Age inclinations is alluded to in *We are the Beloved*. He writes that one of the ways he listens to God is by reading *The Daily Word*—a monthly New Age publication his mother had been giving to him since he was a child:

> Listening, for me, also includes reading other helpful devotional books. In addition to reading the Bible each morning, I usually read a selection from a daily devotional—a collection of inspirational readings

designed to be read through in a year. My current
favorites are *Time With God* and *The Daily Word* (a
monthly publication my mother has given me since
I was a child).[18]

The Daily Word is published in Unity Village, Missouri by the
New Age Unity School of Christianity. Their "Christianity" is
definitely not biblical. In fact, they are long-time proponents of
A Course in Miracles that teaches that "the recognition of God
is the recognition of yourself"[19] and that we are all Christ.[20] As
previously mentioned (on page 38), the Unity School of Christianity is where Robert Schuller told New Age believers about the
need to counter Christian "Fundamentalists" by "positivizing"
the Christian faith.

Norman Vincent Peale and Robert Schuller were both drawn
to the New Age/New Thought "principles" of the Unity School.
Peale said he believed the Unity movement was "good" because it
"has brought the Divine into the consciousness of untold thousands of people."[21] Schuller also showed his adherence to these
Unity "principles" when he said "how helpful they had been to
him in his work."[22]

While Rick Warren and his apologist probably hoped that
the Ken Blanchard "problem" would just quietly disappear,
more New Age implications regarding Blanchard would come
to light. In 1988 when Blanchard really was a new believer—he
co-authored a book with Norman Vincent Peale. The book was
titled *The Power of Ethical Management* and was based on New
Age/self-esteem type principles popularized by Peale and Schuller
through the years. The book was published just two years after
Peale endorsed Bernie Siegel's book *Love, Medicine & Miracles.*

Church Growth: Peale, Schuller, Warren

In his e-mail to Lighthouse Trails, Rick Warren made only one
mention of Norman Vincent Peale in expressing his objections to
George Mair's book. He stated: "Mair says that New Age Minister

Norman Vincent Peale was my mentor!"[23] But as Lighthouse Trails pointed out in their response to Warren, Mair never said that Peale was Rick Warren's "mentor." Mair simply stated that Peale had been instrumental in laying the groundwork for today's Church Growth movement.[24] Robert Schuller, however, has openly described Peale as *his* mentor.[25] And Schuller has described how Peale's 1957 appearance at his church helped to catapult Schuller and his church into prominence. Schuller's megachurch soon inspired the whole Church Growth movement.[26] And while Warren avoids crediting Peale or Schuller for influencing his ministry, there is no doubt that Saddleback Church was forged in the bowels of a Church Growth movement that was inspired by their teachings. Just as clearly as Schuller described Norman Vincent Peale as his mentor, Schuller's Hour of Power website stated that Rick Warren had been "mentored" by Schuller's ministry.[27]

Stumbling into the Truth

Many people felt empathy for George Mair. All he did was write a positive, upbeat account of Rick Warren and his Purpose Driven movement. It was a given that Mair was a popular writer who knew he had a good story in Warren. But the fact of the matter is that he wrote a very flattering account of Warren's life and ministry. He had even subtitled his book—*The Reverend Rick Warren: the Most Inspiring Pastor of Our Time*. While writing his book, Mair had attended Saddleback Church and even contributed money to the church. On paper—book or no book—George Mair would seem to be the kind of person Rick Warren would want to reach out to and try to encourage in the faith. Yet Warren expressed nothing but disdain for this man who had only good things to say about him. Mair had obviously hit a very sensitive nerve with Warren.

What was it about Mair's book that affected Rick Warren so greatly? The objections Warren listed seemed rather trivial and superficial. Was Warren really that upset over whether or not he was described as meeting his wife in high school or college? Or whether or not Warren's father officially headed up a youth ministry? Or were the issues Warren raised masking his real concern regarding Mair's book—how Mair had described Norman Vincent Peale and Robert Schuller as the founding fathers of the modern day Church Growth movement that eventually gave birth to Rick Warren's Saddleback Church and his whole Purpose Driven movement.

Rick Warren protested in his e-mail to Lighthouse Trails that he had never even read Norman Vincent Peale's *The Power of Positive Thinking*. But what Warren was overlooking was that Robert Schuller probably read every book Peale ever wrote and that Schuller had incorporated many of Peale's teachings into his own books and sermons. These teachings were then passed on to pastors, like Warren, who were now passing them on to others whether they realized it or not. In *Deceived on Purpose*, I wrote:

> [I]t seemed that one of Rick Warren's unstated purposes was to mainstream Robert Schuller's teachings into the more traditional "Bible-based" wing of the Church. Many believers who seem to trust Rick Warren, ironically, do not trust Robert Schuller. Rick Warren's "magic" seems to be able to make the teachings of Robert Schuller palatable to believers who would have otherwise never accepted these same teachings had they come directly from Schuller himself.[28]

Whether or not Rick Warren ever read *The Power of Positive Thinking* or ever met one-on-one with Robert Schuller were not the issues. The point George Mair made most effectively in his book was that Warren and the whole Church Growth movement had been greatly influenced by Norman Vincent Peale and Schuller. And this was not something that Rick Warren wanted to see in a book published by Penguin Books and going out to countless numbers of people. Mair's observations have underlined my concern regarding the definite New Age implications to Rick Warren's Purpose Driven movement.

George Mair probably understood very little about New Age teachings. The New Age was probably not something evil or deceptive to him. But in his research, he came upon the *Lutheran Quarterly* article that described Norman Vincent Peale's attraction to New Age teachings. All Mair did was report what he found. He wasn't making any judgment about Peale or the New Age. I knew from a book Mair had previously written about Oprah Winfrey, that he had similarly discovered Oprah's New Age affections and her relationship with New Age leader Marianne Williamson. To Mair, this wasn't a negative thing. It was just part of what turned up in his research. However, by simply doing his homework, Mair had turned over a Norman Vincent Peale-Robert Schuller rock that Warren would have preferred being left alone. Ironically, Mair was just trying to write a positive book about Rick Warren. It just so happened that he stumbled upon the truth.

Christian Charity?

George Mair was stunned by Rick Warren's overwhelmingly negative—even hostile—reaction to his book. It never occurred to Mair that "the most inspiring pastor of our time" would be so offended by the writing of such a favorable book. Prior to the untoward treatment he received from Rick Warren and his apologists, Mair said he had been extremely impressed with Warren and his Purpose Driven ministry. During the writing of his book, Mair said he had come to believe that Rick Warren was a "great man."[29] After *A Life With Purpose* was published, Mair acknowledged he was genuinely shocked by the angry response he received from Warren and his apologist. Commenting specifically on this, George Mair stated:

> I am stunned by the viciousness of the attacks on me
> although I know that sort of thing happens (never

has in my 20 or so previous works). . . . Even more
curious to me is what happened to the concept of
Christian charity. [30]

Two further notes of irony. First, to insure the accuracy of
his book, George Mair wanted to make sure his manuscript was
made available to Rick Warren before it went to press. According
to a written statement Mair provided to Lighthouse Trails, he
contacted Saddleback's "chief attorney," but several months went
by with no response from the attorney. When the Saddleback
attorney finally responded, it was too late—the book had already
gone to press. [31] Secondly, as Warren appeared to distance himself
from Ken Blanchard, Warren was actually sitting on the National
Board of Blanchard's Lead Like Jesus organization and would be
one of the key endorsers of Blanchard's 2005 book, *Lead Like
Jesus*. But even with Saddleback's all-out efforts at damage control, Rick Warren and his staff were about to be embarrassed in
a whole new way by one of Rick Warren's "best friends."

Six

Schuller—The *Real* Leader

> You know it's only if you are a visionary do you know
> the price tag it takes to be the *real* leader, I mean way
> out front on the edge.[1]
>
> —Bruce Wilkinson, Praising Robert Schuller,
> *Hour of Power*, April 24, 2005

On April 24, 2005, five days after the Lighthouse Trails press release regarding Ken Blanchard, Bruce Wilkinson was Robert Schuller's *Hour of Power* guest speaker at the Crystal Cathedral. Wilkinson—the man Rick Warren described as "one of my best friends in the whole world"[2]—led the Crystal Cathedral congregation in a standing ovation for Schuller. He did this after favorably referencing George Mair's newly published book, A *Life with Purpose*, which described Schuller's key role in the formation of today's Church Growth movement. Sidestepping, yet building upon Mair's comments about Norman Vincent Peale, Bruce Wilkinson hailed Robert Schuller as "the grandfather of it all"—"a visionary" and "the *real* leader." Enthusiastically praising Schuller and his Crystal Cathedral, Wilkinson told the congregation:

> I love this church. I love being here. I love walking
> on this property. I just felt like I was one step away
> from heaven when I came on this property this
> morning. I read a book this past week. Somebody

gave it to me, and it traced the past fifty years of Christianity in America and it began to talk about how the transition occurred in our country that eventually led to seeker service, it led to Rick Warren, it led to Bill Hybels and Willow [Creek]. And do you know this book—you probably haven't even seen it yet—this book brought all that back to a person who said this was the grandfather of it all who influenced this person, this person, and this person and from that it became the massive movement it is today. And the person that they named in the book was none other than the pastor of this church. That's amazing ladies and gentlemen! Truly amazing! It is truly amazing! Yes! [The congregation gives Schuller a standing ovation] You know it's only if you are a visionary do you know the price tag it takes to be the *real* leader, I mean way out front on the edge. People like to shoot people on the edge.[3]

But Bruce Wilkinson's strong supportive words stood in stark contrast to the posturing and distancing Rick Warren was attempting to construct between Robert Schuller, Norman Vincent Peale, George Mair's new book, and himself. Wilkinson certainly seemed to have no objections to Schuller or with George Mair's description of a Church Growth movement that was founded by Peale and Schuller. The ironic twist here was that while Warren had supposedly distanced himself from Schuller, one of his "best friends in the whole world," Bruce Wilkinson, was preaching from Schuller's pulpit and calling Schuller "a visionary," and the *real* leader.

The double irony pointed out in *Deceived on Purpose* was that two years earlier, Bruce Wilkinson had come directly from speaking at the Crystal Cathedral one week to speak at Saddleback Church the next week.[4] The theme at both churches was preparing the church for "God's Dream." As already mentioned, "God's

Dream" was a term that Robert Schuller had been popularizing for decades.[5] Wilkinson had come to Saddleback at the request of Rick Warren to help prepare Saddleback Church for the unveiling of Warren's P.E.A.C.E. Plan—the Schulleresque P.E.A.C.E. Plan that Warren just happened to be calling "God's Dream For You—and the World." Yet Warren's Saddleback apologists were now trying to convince everyone that Warren had distanced himself from Schuller.

In July 2005, a hastily written book authored by Richard Abanes, who by that time had moved into the role of Rick Warren's chief apologist, would suddenly seem to answer everyone's questions about Rick Warren. This book, titled *Rick Warren and the Purpose that Drives Him*, was published by Harvest House. Contrary to all publishing standards, this obvious damage-control book was offered free to any pastor in the world requesting a copy. I spoke with a pastor's wife who had called for a free copy of the book. She said a Harvest House representative told her the publishing house had not provided the funding for the free books. The representative stated that the funding came from outside sources associated with the author.[6]

Blanchard "Moves Forward"

In mid-July of 2005, Ken Blanchard posted a statement on his Lead Like Jesus website, admitting that his New Age endorsements were "problematic." He gave his "promise" that he would try to "exercise better discernment in the future."[7] Blanchard stated that a discernment ministry called Watchman Fellowship would "assist" him in becoming more discerning. Three days later, in spite of Blanchard's considerable New Age entanglements and obvious spiritual confusion, Watchman Fellowship announced that Blanchard would remain at the helm of the Lead Like Jesus organization. On July 25, 2005, James Walker—the president of Watchman Fellowship—issued the following statement:

> After spending time with Mr. Blanchard we are now convinced that he is, in fact, a brother in Christ and are committed to assist him as he continues to work through the issues that have arisen as a result of these past endorsements. We encourage you to pray for Ken and the Lead Like Jesus staff as they move forward.[8]

Thus, while George Mair and Lighthouse Trails continued to be heavily criticized by those associated with Rick Warren and Saddleback, Ken Blanchard forged on with his Lead Like Jesus movement. It wasn't too long after this that Blanchard would endorse another New Age book. In January 2006, just six months after the assurance that Watchman Fellowship would be providing oversight and that Blanchard would stop endorsing New Age books, Blanchard endorsed Jon Gordon's *The 10 Minute Energy Solution*.[9] In this book, Gordon favorably quotes and references numerous New Age sources including *A Course in Miracles*, Wayne Dyer, Marilyn Ferguson, Paramahansa Yogananda, and others. The book also points readers to New Age writings by Deepak Chopra, Marianne Williamson, and Gary Zukav. Gordon's New Age-promoting book, bearing Blanchard's endorsement on the cover, was published after Blanchard's own 2005 book—*Lead Like Jesus*—was released. Thus, while Blanchard's book was teaching everyone how to "Lead Like Jesus," the Blanchard-endorsed book by Gordon was simultaneously promoting the New Age "Jesus" who was "another Jesus"—the "Jesus" of the New Age/New Spirituality.

But Ken Blanchard's continued lack of discernment didn't seem to faze Rick Warren or any of the other Christian leaders who so readily supported Blanchard and his Lead Like Jesus book and organization. Nor did Blanchard's persistent New Age affections prevent Rick Warren from continuing to sit on Blanchard's Lead Like Jesus National Board.[10]

Blanchard's Continued Confusion

In a personal interview with Saddleback's Richard Abanes that was published in Abanes' book *Rick Warren and the Purpose that Drives Him*, Rick Warren offered an additional line of defense regarding Ken Blanchard's New Age sympathies. By all appearances, Rick Warren had distanced himself from Blanchard—just as had been the case with Robert Schuller. Warren stated that Blanchard was not a "deep Christian" and that he had recently told Blanchard "You started in ministry *before* you got to maturity." Continuing to emphasize Blanchard's immaturity as a believer, Warren stated: "He just needs to be taken aside and instructed in the ways of the Lord."[11] But what Warren did not mention in the interview was why he would endorse Blanchard's book, *Lead Like Jesus*, sit on Blanchard's Lead Like Jesus National Board, and let someone who was "not a deep Christian" and "who needs to be instructed in the ways of the Lord" play such an important role in the Purpose Driven P.E.A.C.E. Plan. How could Rick Warren ever expect someone lacking Christian maturity to train countless people around the world to "lead like Jesus?"

Ken Blanchard's on-going New Age affections have been carefully documented by ministries like Christian Research Service and Lighthouse Trails Publishing. For example, in 2007 Blanchard provided a new foreword and his continued endorsement for Jim Ballard's New Age book *Little Wave and Old Swell*. Then, in early 2008, Blanchard was one of the featured speakers at a Southern California conference that was highlighting the New Age book *The Secret*.[12] Incidentally, he spoke at the same event in 2009 as well, sharing a platform with some of the most prolific New Age authors today, including Wayne Dyer, John Gray, and Mark Victor Hansen. And in 2008, Blanchard's endorsement was on the front cover of another book by New Age sympathizer Jon Gordon.[13] He has also remained a member of the Advisory Council of the New Age-based Hoffman Institute,[14] an organization that promotes the Hoffman Quadrinity Process. The Quadrinity Process was devised by psychic Robert Hoffman[15] and is based on the foundational New Age belief that God is "in" everything.

Rick Warren's involvement with Ken Blanchard cannot be conveniently excused and explained away. His association with Blanchard is symptomatic of a Purpose Driven ship without scriptural bearings.

> For the time will come when they will not endure sound doctrine; but after their own lusts shall they heap to themselves teachers, having itching ears; And they shall turn away their ears from the truth, and shall be turned unto fables. (2 Timothy 4:3-4)

One further note regarding Ken Blanchard and his Lead Like Jesus campaign. In a radio interview with WMKL in Miami, Florida, Blanchard, as the author of *The One Minute Manager*, recounted a visit he had had with Robert Schuller at the Crystal Cathedral. Schuller had told him that Jesus was the "greatest one-minute manager of all time." Blanchard said in the interview that it was after this Schuller remark that for "the first time I started thinking of Jesus as a leader."[16]

Much like Rick Warren's reference to Bernie Siegel in *The Purpose Driven Life*, Warren's association with Ken Blanchard was just one more in a string of New Age implications that have yet to be adequately accounted for. With that said, it is important to take a moment to revisit the Bernie Siegel matter more completely.

Seven

Bernie Siegel Revisited

> Dr. Bernie Siegel in his book *Love, Medicine, and Miracles* writes: . . . Anything that offers hope . . . has the potential to heal.[1]
>
> —Robert Schuller, 1989

As I described in *Deceived on Purpose*, one of the early clues about Robert Schuller's pervasive, overlapping influence on Rick Warren's ministry was Warren's seemingly out of the blue reference to Bernie Siegel. In his book *The Purpose Driven Life*, Warren suddenly and indiscriminately referenced Siegel regarding the subjects of "hope" and "purpose." He did this without warning his readers that Siegel was a New Age leader with a spirit guide named "George." In his 1986 book *Love, Medicine & Miracles*, Siegel described how he had contacted "George" the very first time he meditated.[2]

I also described that I had discovered that thirteen years before Rick Warren referenced Bernie Siegel regarding "hope" and "purpose," Schuller had referenced Siegel in regard to this same theme in a 1989 book titled *Believe in the God who Believes in You*.[3] On his *Hour of Power* television program, Schuller had even described the New Age Siegel as "one of the greatest doctors of the 20th Century."[4] Siegel, in turn, was one of the prominent front-page endorsers of Robert Schuller's 1995 book *Prayer: My Soul's Adventure with God: A Spiritual Autobiography*. Rick Warren's reference to Siegel is probably what Saddleback apologist Gilbert Thurston referred to as certain things Warren "learned from the books of Robert Schuller."[5]

To try to distance Rick Warren from the reality of Schuller's obvious mentoring influence, Saddleback apologist Richard Abanes wrote that it was actually Baptist preacher W. A. Criswell—not Schuller—who mentored Rick Warren. Abanes wrote:

> If anyone can be credited with being his [Rick Warren's] spiritual mentor and model, it would be this stalwart of Christianity.[6]

But Abanes' attempt to deflect attention away from Robert Schuller and over to W. A. Criswell ended up backfiring on him. In 1995, Criswell not only endorsed and wrote the foreword to Rick Warren's book *The Purpose Driven Church*, but he also endorsed Schuller's book *Prayer: My Soul's Adventure with God*. Criswell's endorsement was just several endorsements below that of Dr. Bernie Siegel. The irony of Abanes' attempt to deflect attention away from Schuller via Criswell is that Criswell leads right back to Schuller. Criswell's endorsement of Schuller's book actually turned out to be a blanket endorsement of *anything* that Schuller had ever written. Criswell wrote:

> Anything the world-famous preacher/pastor Robert Schuller writes is fascinating and inspiring to the whole world. How much more so when the book concerns his soul's adventure with God.[7]

W. A. Criswell, the "mentor" Rick Warren referred to as his "father in ministry,"[8] and C. Peter Wagner, the "mentor" Warren had for his doctoral dissertation,[9] both had such high regard for Robert Schuller,[10] it is not surprising that Schuller has had so much influence on Rick Warren's ministry. And it is also not surprising that Norman Vincent Peale, Schuller's self-professed mentor, was also involved with Bernie Siegel. Peale's prominent endorsement was featured on the back cover of Bernie Siegel's *Love, Medicine & Miracles*. This Peale-Schuller-Warren connection to Siegel criss-crosses and intersects in such a way as to make the interconnection between the three of them undeniable.

Not Mentored by Schuller?

In Richard Abanes' interview with Rick Warren that was included in Abanes' book *Rick Warren and the Purpose that Drives Him*, Warren gave the distinct impression he had little or no regard for Robert Schuller. In fact, Schuller seemed to be almost a persona non grata to Warren with no mentoring influence in his life at all. When asked if Schuller was his mentor, Warren emphatically stated: "*No! Never has been, never would be!*"[11] This response seemed consistent with his May 31, 2005 e-mail to Lighthouse Trails where he made it appear he hardly even knew Schuller—thus implying that Schuller could not have ever had any mentoring influence in his life. Rick Warren's e-mail had stated:

> I have never even had a private one-on-one conversation with Mr. Schuller—ever![12]

Yet in a 1995 presentation with New Age sympathizer/Methodist pastor Leonard Sweet, Rick Warren told Sweet that he had been "mentored" by people he had never even met by reading their books. Warren told Sweet:

> I have read dozens and dozens and dozens of books. People have mentored me that I have never met.[13]

Given the obvious influence that Schuller's writings and teachings have had on Rick Warren, one has to wonder why Warren would go to such great lengths to deny the influence of someone whose words, thoughts, and ideas so completely permeate his ministry. In the "Acknowledgments" of *The Purpose Driven Life,* Warren seems so generous when he writes:

> I am grateful to the hundreds of writers and teachers, both classical and contemporary, who have shaped my life and helped me learn these truths.[14]

Whether or not Rick Warren describes Robert Schuller as his "mentor," are we to believe that Schuller is not one of the "hundreds of writers and teachers" who shaped and influenced Rick Warren's life? But to read Richard Abanes' "interview" with Rick Warren, it would seem that Schuller has had no significant influence on Rick Warren's ministry. Yet this simply isn't true. Again, Saddleback apologist Gilbert Thurston told a much different story than the one being told by Rick Warren and Richard Abanes when he stated: "There is no question that Robert Schuller has been an influence on Rick through the years."[15] And while Saddleback apologists have tried in a number of different ways to deflate Kay Warren's statement in a 2002 *Christianity Today* interview, she made it very clear that Robert Schuller had greatly influenced her husband. She stated: "He had a profound influence on Rick . . . We were captivated by his positive appeal to nonbelievers."[16]

Yet in *Rick Warren and The Purpose that Drives Him,* Richard Abanes indicates that Warren separated himself theologically from Robert Schuller back in 1998—as if that explained away all of the Schuller influence that is still so present in Rick Warren's ministry today.[17] And even if the theological separation was really true, a reasonable question would be, "What took Rick Warren so long to separate himself from Schuller? Discerning believers have been exposing Schuller's false teachings for over five decades—ever since Schuller's ministry was jump started by Norman Vincent Peale in 1957.[18] This would imply that Richard Abanes is saying that for twenty-four years—from the time Rick Warren read his first Schuller book in 1974[19] all the way to 1998—Rick Warren believed that Schuller had a sound godly ministry. In fact, in his 1995 book *The*

Purpose Driven Church, Rick Warren lists Schuller's church as one of "many strong, Bible-believing churches" in Southern California.[20] This statement alone reflects the tremendous influence Schuller has exerted over thousands of pastors like Rick Warren through the years—pastors who have read his books, availed themselves of his teachings, and graduated from his Institute for Successful Church Leadership. It also reflects the amazing lack of discernment of so many of today's pastors. And while Rick Warren supposedly separated himself from Schuller in 1998, recent printings of his book *The Purpose Driven Church* still list Schuller's Crystal Cathedral as one of "many strong, Bible-believing churches" in Southern California.[21]

Covey, Strobel, Kay Warren, and Schuller

Richard Abanes writes that it is because Mormon Stephen Covey spoke at the Crystal Cathedral in 1998 that Rick Warren separated himself from Schuller and has since refused all speaking invitations from Schuller.[22] Schuller allowing Mormon Stephen Covey to speak at the Crystal Cathedral is the reason given for the separation. On paper, this seems to indicate that Warren has a real problem with Covey. Yet, Kenny Luck, the men's pastor at Saddleback Church, nonchalantly quotes Stephen Covey in his 2007 book *Dream*. He quotes Covey to make an important point about fulfilling "God's Dream."[23] The irony is that Luck— a Saddleback pastor—is using the Mormon Covey—the man who supposedly caused Warren to separate himself theologically from Schuller—to underscore the Schuller concept of "God's Dream" that both Warren and Kenny Luck are pushing.

Another case in point. Though Rick Warren has been theoretically separated from Robert Schuller since 1998, he apparently had no problem with one of his own Saddleback pastors—Lee Strobel— speaking at Schuller's 2002 Institute for Successful Church Leadership. Strobel was a Saddleback pastor under Rick Warren at that time.[24] In another more recent instance, Rick Warren's wife, Kay, was a featured speaker at Schuller's well-publicized 2008 "Rethink Conference" held at the Crystal Cathedral.[25] Rick Warren had to be aware that Kay Warren's appearance with Schuller would reinforce the idea that Schuller was still a respected and acceptable Christian leader. This obviously contradicted the "separation" stance Warren was trying to project through his Saddleback apologists. As Kay Warren spoke, Rick Warren's apologists were on record describing Schuller as someone who had "gotten off the track of traditional Christianity,"[26] was "universalistic,"[27] a "heretic-liberal,"[28] and one of the "*true* New Agers."[29] Yet there was Schuller holding court at his Crystal Cathedral Rethink Conference with speakers Kay Warren and Rick Warren colleagues Lee Strobel, Charles Colson, Erwin McManus, and others. There was a time when believers would not even think of speaking at a conference that was hosted by a New Age sympathizing Christian leader. In an article I wrote about Schuller's 2008 Rethink Conference, I stated the obvious:

> While Rick Warren has tried desperately to deny his spiritual ties to Schuller, his wife's presence at the conference speaks volumes.[30]

Robert Schuller's Rethink Conference–supposedly a platform for Christian and world leaders to "grapple" with world problems–seemed to be a perfect vehicle for keeping Schuller in the thick of things. As Kay Warren spoke at the Rethink Conference, Schuller's 2005 book, *Don't Throw Away Tomorrow: Living God's Dream For Your Life* was available for purchase by conference attendees. With a back cover endorsement by New Age leader Gerald Jampolsky, Schuller's book described "God's Dream," world peace, and Schuller's strong belief in "the healing quality of wise compromise."[31]

If Rick Warren was concerned about Stephen Covey's appearance at the Crystal Cathedral, what about Gerald Jampolsky's *Hour of Power* appearance in October 2004?[32] With his wife, Kay, speaking at Schuller's conference, Rick Warren's political posturing with Schuller was obvious to all those who had the eyes to see and the ears to hear what was really going on.

Grievous Wolves

Scripture is very clear that we are to "have no fellowship with the unfruitful works of darkness, but rather reprove them" (Ephesians 5:11). If the apostle Paul had been married, he definitely would not have sent his wife off to an Alexander the Coppersmith Rethink Conference to help solve world problems. Rather he would do just what he did—name names, expose evil, and warn the church about men like Alexander the Coppersmith (2 Timothy 4:14-15) and Robert Schuller. The apostle Paul had no patience with the grievous wolves of his time. He warned about them night and day with tears:

> For I have not shunned to declare unto you all the counsel of God. Take heed therefore unto yourselves, and to all the flock, over the which the Holy Ghost hath made you overseers, to feed the church of God, which he hath purchased with his own blood. For I know this, that after my departing shall grievous wolves enter in among you, not sparing the flock. Also of your own selves shall men arise, speaking perverse things, to draw away disciples after them. Therefore watch, and remember, that by the space of three years I ceased not to warn every one night and day with tears. (Acts 20:27-31)

Eight

"God's Dream": A Deceptive Scheme?

I am not fully forgiven until I allow God to write his new dream for my life on the blackboard of my mind . . . God has a great plan to redeem society. He needs me and wants to use me.[1]

—Robert Schuller, 1982

THIS WEEKEND, I'll begin a series of five messages on God's dream to use you globally—to literally use YOU to help change the world![2]

—Rick Warren, 2003

I live inside God's dream for me. . . . God can dream a bigger dream for you than you can dream for yourself.[3]

—Oprah Winfrey, 2006

So people interested in being a new kind of Christian will . . . want to find out how they can fit in with God's dreams actually coming true down here more often.[4]

—Brian McLaren, 2007

"God's Dream" is a term Robert Schuller adopted years ago and has popularized for more than thirty-five years. As previously mentioned, it appears that Rick Warren first encountered the Schuller concept of "God's Dream" in 1974 as a twenty year-old. Six years before he started Saddleback Church, he read Schuller's 1974 book *Your Church Has Real Possibilities*.[5]

In the last chapter of his book, Schuller introduced the term "God's Dream" in his exhortation and charge to budding young pastors. In the chapter titled "How You Can Dream Great Dreams" Schuller writes:

> How do possibility thinkers dream their dreams? Here's how—just follow these three steps as you plan, pray and prepare to become a great leader to build a great church for Jesus Christ:

> He [God] has a dream for your life and your church. He will reveal His dream by causing you to desire what He wants. Prayerfully ask God to fill your life full with His Holy Spirit . . .

> Now pray the prayer of surrender, "God I'm willing to do and be whatever you want me to be. I'm yours to command." Then ask the Holy Spirit to fill your mind with God's dream for your life.

> Big beautiful dreams will come . . .

> Listen to this dream, "For it is God at work within you, giving you the will and the power to achieve His purpose" (Phil. 2:13, *Phillips*). Now . . .

> Show them your dream. . . .

> So, friend, dream your dreams and make them great! I have every confidence that you are about to turn a corner in your ministry . . .

> Why am I so sure? Because the principles of success are all here. You've already read them. Now believe them and apply them. They will work, if you work them!

> And if this is done, the Twentieth Century church
> in America will see a fantastic future unfold before
> it as it moves into the Twenty-First Century.[6]

As Robert Schuller finished his exhortation and concluded his book, the young Rick Warren read:

> Some reader of this book will build the greatest
> church ever built in America . . . It will be a sensation
> for Christ![7]

In this 1974 Schuller book, Rick Warren was introduced not only to Schuller's concept of "God's Dream," but also to Schuller's admiration for Norman Vincent Peale and Peale's book *The Power of Positive Thinking*. Schuller wrote that it was Peale's landmark appearance at his drive-in theater church that launched Schuller's worldwide ministry.[8] I reviewed what Schuller wrote about Peale and "God's Dream," and Schuller's instruction to "work" the "principles of success":

> [T]he principles of success are all here . . . Now
> believe them and apply them. They will work, if
> you work them![9]

Recognizing these New Age principles of occult manifestation from my own days in the New Age, I looked again at Norman Vincent Peale's endorsement of Florence Scovel Shinn's occult/New Age book *The Game of Life*. Peale had written:

> THE GAME OF LIFE is filled with wisdom and
> creative insights. That its teachings will work I know
> to be fact, for I've long used them myself.

> By studying and practicing the principles laid down
> in this book one may find prosperity, solve problems,
> have better health, achieve good personal relations—
> in a word, win the game of life.[10]

Robert Schuller had simply adopted the occult/New Age principles Norman Vincent Peale had adopted from Shinn and other New Age writers. Schuller renamed these principles "possibility thinking" and used the metaphor of "God's Dream" to customize the metaphysical/New Age techniques. It is no wonder that Neale Donald Walsch commended both Peale and Schuller as "extraordinary" Christian ministers: they were presenting New Age teachings on how to create your own reality through occult manifestation. As previously cited, Walsch had written:

> This phenomenon [occult manifestation] is discussed with extraordinary insight in the classic book *The Power of Positive Thinking*, written over fifty years ago by the Reverend Dr. Norman Vincent Peale, a Christian minister who understood that feelings are a gift from God, giving us the power of creation.[11]

Norman Vincent Peale's adapted approach from occultist Florence Scovel Shinn encouraged his readers to "prayerize," "picturize," "actualize"[12] to create what they wanted—to create their own reality so they could be successful. Schuller used slightly different wording to encourage people to dream "God's Dream" to obtain their desires, or in the case of pastors, to create "successful" churches and to make their churches grow. In his book *The Purpose Driven Church*, Rick Warren referenced Schuller's book *Your Church Has Real Possibilities* to describe a Schuller canvassing technique he used in starting Saddleback Church.[13] Warren also used the occult/New Age/Peale/Schuller technique of confidently picturing and affirming future success before it happens. Warren made his affirmations by publicly declaring Saddleback's future success in a series of dream statements patterned after Robert Schuller.[14]

Schuller continues to use the term "God's Dream" today. "God's Dream" is the subtitle of his 2005 book—*Don't Throw Away Tomorrow: Living God's Dream for Your Life*. As already mentioned, that book has a back cover endorsement by Gerald Jampolsky—the man who introduced me to the New Age teachings of *A Course in Miracles*. And Rick Warren chose to use the term "God's Dream"—above all others—to describe his worldwide Purpose Driven P.E.A.C.E. Plan. In an e-mail announcing his P.E.A.C.E. Plan, he called the P.E.A.C.E. Plan "God's Dream For You—And The World!"[15] But Jesus never talked about living your dreams or imagining your dreams. In *Deceived on Purpose*, I wrote:

> When the Bible says that in the last days "your old men shall dream dreams" it isn't talking about these kinds of ["God's Dream"] dreams. The only dreams mentioned in the Bible are dreams that occur during sleep. Biblical dreams and visions have *nothing* to do with those that are imagined and found in men's hearts [the kind of "dreams" that Robert Schuller, the New Age, and a deceived church were conceiving].[16]

More Saddleback Spin

Rick Warren's use of Robert Schuller's "God's Dream" metaphor is another one of the many issues that have not been straight-forwardly addressed by Warren and his Saddleback apologists. They have avoided dealing with the fact that the term "God's Dream" is an unbiblical Schuller concept. Rather than dealing directly with that fact, Warren's apologists simply isolated the single word "dream" instead. They made it appear that I was saying that the word "dream"—not "God's Dream"—was unbiblical and that I was wrong in taking Warren to task for using the term "dream." With this damage-control strategy, the word "dream" became the issue, not Warren's use of the Schuller term "God's Dream" to describe his P.E.A.C.E. Plan. By not identifying the real issue—the term "God's Dream" and its linkage to Schuller—they simply argued that the single word "dream" was a biblical concept. This, of course, made my argument look foolish to the reader who was relying on Saddleback's integrity to accurately describe my concerns. In his "Response to *Deceived on Purpose* by Warren Smith," Saddleback apologist Gilbert Thurston wrote:

> As for the word dream, Mr. Smith is technically correct when he says that every time the word dream is used in the Bible it's referring to sleeping dreams or waking visions. However, he's incorrect when he tries to imply that the kind of dreams that Rick Warren, Bruce Wilkinson or even Robert Schuller, for that matter, talk about are not found in the Bible.[17]

Thus, the full phrase "God's Dream" was avoided altogether. Saddleback apologist, Richard Abanes, took it one step further. Also avoiding any mention of the term "God's Dream," he suggested that Warren's reference was patterned more after Martin Luther King's "I have a Dream" speech than Robert Schuller. He wrote:

> Smith plays the same word game with "dream"—a term used by both Rick Warren and Robert Schuller. . . . [Rick] Warren has talked about his dream for the P.E.A.C.E. Plan. And Schuller has often used the word *dream* in his teachings regarding church leadership, church growth, and New Age concepts. But that does NOT mean the two men are using the word in the same way.
>
> In fact, Warren's use of the word "dream" dates all the way back to his first sermon at Saddleback in 1980 (BEFORE Schuller's 1982 book *Self-Esteem: A [sic] New Reformation*). He listed several dreams he had for his church. And, in my opinion, it is more reminiscent of Martin Luther King's "I have a Dream" speech in Washington D.C. than anything Schuller has ever said/written.[18]

But these two Saddleback apologists were the ones playing the word games. In this second example with Richard Abanes, the single word "dream" was again substituted for the actual phrase in question—"God's Dream." Also, this apologist never addressed the real issue of Rick Warren's specific use of the Robert Schuller term "God's Dream" in describing his Global P.E.A.C.E. Plan. Just like Gilbert Thurston, he tried to contain the discussion to the more generic and easily defensible term "dream." Then when he argues that Warren's use of the term "dream" in his first Saddleback sermon in 1980 was "more reminiscent of Martin Luther King's 'I Have a Dream' speech," he overlooks the fact that in 1980 Warren had just graduated from The Robert H. Schuller Institute for Successful Church Leadership where—according to Kay Warren—her husband had been profoundly influenced by Robert Schuller.[19] Abanes also overlooks the fact that in Warren's book *The Purpose Driven Church*, Warren had written that six years before he founded Saddleback Church, he had read Schuller's book *Your Church has Real Possibilities*. In this book, Schuller made several references to the term "God's Dream" before he issued the following challenge to young pastors near the end of his book:

> You've got to believe it before you see it! So believe you can build a Twenty-First Century church now! You can be the founder and the leader of such a great new inspirational center. You can make your church a great church for Jesus Christ.[20]

> Some reader of this book will build the greatest church ever built in America.[21]

Saddleback apologists completely avoided what had been so clearly described in *Deceived on Purpose*—the fact that Rick Warren's use of the term "God's Dream" was directly related to Robert Schuller. But the Schuller term "God's Dream" doesn't stop with Rick Warren. It now stretches into the worldwide church and into the New Age itself. The concept that Schuller popularized over the years is becoming a frequently used metaphor for world peace. It seems obvious from all the spin that Saddleback apologists did not want to advertise the fact that the "God's Dream" metaphor Rick Warren used to describe his P.E.A.C.E. Plan was a term that Schuller had been using and popularizing for over thirty-five years.

"God's Dream" and Brian McLaren

In his 2006 book *The Secret Message of Jesus: Uncovering the Truth That Could Change Everything*, alternative emerging church figure Brian McLaren proposes that Christians adopt new metaphors that the church can use to introduce the world to Jesus—a new user-friendly language to more effectively communicate with the prevailing culture of a "postmodern" world. The first new metaphor that McLaren suggests is the old Robert Schuller metaphor, "God's Dream." And like Abanes, McLaren tries to link this Schuller concept to Martin Luther King's "I have a Dream" speech rather than attributing it to Schuller. McLaren explains:

> For all these reasons, "the dream of God" strikes me as a beautiful way to translate the message of the kingdom of God for hearers today. It is, of course, the language evoked by Dr. Martin Luther King Jr. as he stood on the steps of the Lincoln Memorial on August 28, 1963. His dream was God's dream, and that accounted for its amazing power.[22]

It is significant to note that using the Schuller "God's Dream" metaphor and then linking it with Martin Luther King's civil rights movement and King's "I have a Dream" speech are what many church and New Age leaders are presently doing. It is part of the emerging "merging" process going on. New Age leaders are linking the New Age Peace Plan—what they are now calling their "civil rights movement for the soul"[23]—to the same Martin Luther King "I have a Dream" speech. Marianne Williamson's Peace Alliance—formerly the Global Renaissance Alliance of New Age leaders—even has a poster with Martin Luther King's picture featured on their website.* The poster proclaims that "One Dream Can Change Everything."[24] As described in *Deceived on Purpose,* Marianne Williamson's New Age colleague Wayne Dyer has made it clear that the "One Dream" that can change everything is "God's Dream":

> Who is the ultimate dreamer? Call it as you will: God, higher consciousness, Krishna, Spirit, whatever pleases you. . . .
>
> One dream, one dreamer, billions of embodied characters acting out that one dream . . . Your true essence is that you are part and parcel of the one big dream.[25]
>
> This is the quintessential message that is available from all the spiritual masters . . . You, the dreamer . . . God, the dreamer.[26]
>
> I assure you that when you truly know that there is only one dream and that you are connected to everyone in that dream, you begin to think and act as if you are connected to it all, rather than attached to your separateness.[27]

Linking "God's Dream" with Martin Luther King's "I have a Dream" speech is a clever device that touches a deep emotional pocket within most people. This, in turn, opens them up spiritually to whatever teaching is being pushed—such as "we are all one" because God is "in" everything. This whole Schuller "God's

---

* The poster has two photos on it: Martin Luther King and Gandhi.

Dream"/Martin Luther King/"I have a Dream" device is being used to create a false sense of togetherness and unity—to bring everyone together psychologically and spiritually as "One."

An Internet search could find no instance of Martin Luther King ever using the term "God's Dream." It is Robert Schuller—not Martin Luther King—who has popularized the term "God's Dream" over the years. It is no wonder that Marianne Williamson's colleague Neale Donald Walsch is so eager to describe Schuller as an "extraordinary minister" and someone who could help create a bridge between the church and the New Age with his God "in" everyone "God's Dream" theology of self-esteem. In *Self-Esteem: The New Reformation*—the 1982 book that obviously inspired both Rick Warren and Neale Donald Walsch—Schuller wrote:

> Tremendous human energy is needed to walk God's walk, work God's work, fulfill God's will, and complete his dream for our self-esteem.[28]

Saddleback Men's Ministry

If there is any doubt about Rick Warren and Saddleback's continued use of the Robert Schuller term "God's Dream," simply read Saddleback men's pastor Kenny Luck's 2007 book—*Dream: Have You Caught God's Vision?* and his accompanying *Dream Workbook*. Both books use the term "God's Dream" throughout their texts. In *Dream*, Kenny Luck sounds a lot like Schuller and Norman Vincent Peale when he concludes the foreword by writing—"Dreaming big with you." Here is a brief sampling of that Saddleback pastor's use of the term "God's Dream":

> God's dream for us is dangerously attractive, inviting, and controversial.[29]

> My prayer is that as you, and several of your friends,

grapple with the content of this workbook, God's dream for your life will erupt for His glory and the advancement of the cause of Christ. Our world desperately needs men living out the dreams God has burned into their hearts.[30]

God's dream for you is a heaven-owned vision of greatness, a God's man image built upon that of the God-Man.[31]

God's dream is to see you reach that summit.[32]

Five years after Rick Warren introduced his P.E.A.C.E. Plan as "God's Dream For You—And The World!," Robert Schuller's metaphor continues to be emphasized by a wide cross-section of church and New Age leaders. Even Oprah Winfrey is using the term.[33]

The Spiritual Trap

Using the term "God's Dream" and other overlapping transformational language, Rick Warren's ever-evolving Global P.E.A.C.E. Plan is in the process of semantically merging with the PEACE Plan of the New Age/New Spirituality. "God's Dream" has become the "Pied Piper" *Field of Dreams* rallying cry for a deceptive world peace plan that purports to establish the kingdom of God here on earth through humanitarian effort and global good works.

But "God's Dream," as described by its proponents cannot and will not succeed. It is not a case of "if you build it, he will come."[34] While humanity is to always do its best in meeting human and environmental needs, the kingdom of God will not be established by humanity imagining and creating world peace by invoking a Schulleresque New Age"God's Dream" PEACE Plan. The kingdom of God comes just as prophesied in the Bible—through the return of our Lord and Savior Jesus

Christ—the real Jesus Christ—not the false Christ of a deceived and apostate church. Not the false Christ of a New Age/New Spirituality.

> Behold, I am against them that prophesy false dreams, saith the LORD, and do tell them, and cause my people to err by their lies, and by their lightness; yet I sent them not, nor commanded them: therefore they shall not profit this people at all, saith the LORD. (Jeremiah 23:32)

Who's Talking About "God's Dream"?

Church Leaders

Now—find God's dream for your life and go all out for it![1]
—**Robert Schuller**

On October 18-19 [2003], I shared God's dream for our church locally. On October [27-28], Bruce Wilkinson shared God's dream for us individually. THIS WEEKEND, I'll begin a series of five messages on God's dream to use you globally - to literally use YOU to help change the world. I'll unveil our Global P.E.A.C.E. plan, and how God has uniquely prepared you for this moment of destiny.[2]—**Rick Warren**

When you begin to create the life of your dreams—or maybe better stated, when you begin to live the life that God dreams for you—you take responsibility to prepare for the future.[3]—**Erwin McManus**

You have been handcrafted by God to accomplish a part of His Big Dream for the world.[4]—**Bruce Wilkinson**

The end of war begins with people who believe that another world is possible and that another empire has already interrupted time and space and is taking over this earth with the dreams of God.[5]—**Shane Claiborne**

The time to save God's Dream is now. The people to save God's Dream are you.[6]—**Leonard Sweet**

That in itself is an act of peacemaking, because we're seeking to align our wills with God's will, our dreams with God's dream.[7]—**Brian McLaren**

Who's Talking About "God's Dream"?

New Age/New Spirituality Leaders

Just start on your journey upward, inward and forward-upward to see God's Dream, inward to possess God's Dream, forward to become God's Dream. This Dream is the Dream of absolute Fulfillment.[8]—**Sri Chinmoy**

God says, 'Please, please help me realize this dream." And some of God's best collaborators are the young, because you dream. You dream God's dream.[9]—**Desmond Tutu**

God's dream still remains unfulfilled. It was not fulfilled 2,000 years ago, or in the home of any religious leader or any American home, and today the Unification Church is here to pledge to fulfill that dream. We don't want to confine that fulfillment to our Church, but to expand it all over the world. Wouldn't that be the Kingdom of God on earth?[10] —**Sun Myung Moon**

Who is the ultimate dreamer? Call it as you will: God, higher consciousness, Krishna, spirit, whatever pleases you ... One dream, one dreamer, billions of embodied characters acting out that one dream ... Your true essence is that you are part and parcel of the one big dream.[11]—**Wayne Dyer**

I live inside God's dream for me. I don't try to tell God what I'm supposed to do ... God can dream a bigger dream for you than you can dream for yourself.[12]—**Oprah Winfrey**

Nine

Rick Warren and Prophecy Revisited

Blessed is he that readeth, and they that hear the words of this prophecy, and keep those things which are written therein: for the time is at hand.

—**Revelation 1:3**

Prophesy ye not, say they to them that prophesy.

—**Micah 2:6**

Rick Warren openly discourages readers of *The Purpose Driven Life* from studying prophecy. Taking unwarranted and unbiblical liberty in interpreting Acts 1:6-8, he states that Jesus told His disciples that the details of His return "are none of your business"—that they needed to focus on "fulfilling" their "mission" rather than "figuring out prophecy." He writes:

> When the disciples wanted to talk about prophecy, Jesus quickly switched the conversation to evangelism. He wanted them to concentrate on their mission in the world. He said in essence, *"The details of my return are none of your business. What is your business is the mission I've given you. Focus on that! . . ."*

If you want Jesus to come back sooner, *focus on fulfilling your mission*, not figuring out prophecy.[1] (emphasis added)

In 2006, four years after *The Purpose Driven Life* was published, emerging church figure Brian McLaren also used this same interpretation of Acts 1:6-8 to similarly discourage his readers from studying prophecy. Echoing Warren's words, McLaren states the following:

Instead, he [Jesus] tells them it's *none of their business* to speculate about how God plans to work out history, and then he *gives them a mission to accomplish.*[2] (emphasis added)

C. Peter Wagner, Rick Warren's former doctoral "mentor" at Fuller Theological Seminary,[3] explains that what Warren and Brian McLaren were saying is actually what Robert Schuller has been teaching for years. Wagner points out that Schuller is a "pioneer of focusing on the mission of the church" rather than prophecy (eschatology). Wagner writes:

A pioneer of focusing on the *mission* of the church to the surrounding world is Robert H. Schuller, founder of the Crystal Cathedral of Garden Grove, California.[4] (emphasis added, italics in original)

Robert Schuller's advice to young church leaders would seem to apply to new apostolic Christians: "*Don't let eschatology stifle your long-term thinking.*"[5] (emphasis added)

In a curious play on the words "New Age" and "mission" Robert Schuller concludes his 1982 book *Self-Esteem: The New Reformation* by describing how he believes that the twenty-first century would be a "new Age of mission":

> I believe that today we are witnessing the last days
> of the Reactionary Age in church history. And I'm
> further convinced that we are witnessing the birth
> of a new Age of Mission.[6]

But Rick Warren, Brian McLaren, and Robert Schuller are simply repeating what New Age matriarch Alice Bailey received from her spirit guide, Djwhal Khul, concerning the coming of a universal New Age "Christ." In Bailey's 1948 book *The Reappearance of the Christ*, in a chapter titled "Preparation for the Reappearance of the Christ," Bailey writes:

> If our work is rightly done, He will come at the set
> and appointed time. How, where or when He will
> come is *none of our concern.* Our work is to do our
> utmost and on as large a scale as possible to bring
> about right human relations, for His coming *depends
> upon our work.*[7] (emphasis added)

More than fifty years after Alice Bailey channeled these New Age teachings regarding the coming of the New Age "Christ," Rick Warren and Brian McLaren were saying almost the exact same thing. Bailey said the details of "Christ's" return were "none of our concern." Warren and McLaren said that the details of Christ's return were none of our "business." Alice Bailey said that "His coming depends upon our work," while Warren stated "If you want Jesus to come back sooner, focus on fulfilling your mission." All three of them emphasized human endeavor to build the kingdom of God. And all three of them discouraged understanding the details of Christ's return. Yet on the Mount of Olives, the real Jesus Christ went to great lengths to describe the details of His return (Matthew 24, Mark 13, and Luke 21). He shared important details of His return with His disciples so they—and we—would not get deceived by a false Christ—like Alice Bailey's New Age Christ. He did not tell them that the details of His return were "none of their business." He said, "Take heed that no man deceive you" (Matthew 24:4). To make sure they would not be deceived by a false Christ, he went on to provide important details concerning His return. He warned them that "many false prophets shall rise, and shall deceive many" (Matthew 24:11). He also warned:

> Then if any man shall say unto you, Lo, here is Christ, or there; believe it not. For there shall arise false Christs, and false prophets, and shall shew great signs and wonders; insomuch that, if it were possible, they shall deceive the very elect. Behold, I have told you before. (Matthew 24:23-25).

By providing these and other details, Jesus was saying—in essence—don't be deceived by those who tell you that the details of my return are none of your business. On the contrary, Jesus told His disciples that the details of His return are of great importance and that prophecy should be properly understood (Matthew 24:15). Furthermore, in Matthew 24, Mark 13, and Luke 21 Jesus gives a much different picture of what the last days before His return will be like. The leaders I have discussed seem to suggest that if we fulfill our "mission" or "God's Dream" we will create a world where peace prevails. They believe Christ will then return to a world ready to accept Him. But the real Jesus warns that false Christs will appear (leading eventually to the Antichrist)—and they will perform signs and wonders, promising peace and harmony.

My original concern about the New Age implications of Rick Warren's discouragement to study prophecy was further heightened as similar statements by Brian McLaren, Robert Schuller, and New Age matriarch Alice Bailey came to light. Adding to this concern was the fact that emerging church leaders like McLaren, Tony Jones, and others were teaching that the prophecies and predictions in Matthew 24 and Revelation had already been fulfilled by 70 A.D. (preterism).[8] This kind of false teaching is part of the very deception that Jesus was warning His disciples to beware of. This kind of false teaching makes the study of endtime events irrelevant and opens the door to a false New Age Christ and even further deception.

Jihadist Jesus?

In his book *Everything Must Change*, Brian McLaren writes that there are other "Jesus" figures that are being presented as "Jesus" who are not the real Jesus Christ. But rather than exposing the blasphemous false Christ of the New Age/New Spirituality/New World Religion, McLaren describes the "second coming" Christ of the Bible as a false Christ. He describes the "second-coming" Jesus looked for by literal Bible-believers as a "trick Jesus," a "fake-me-out Messiah"—a "jihadist Jesus." He writes:

> The phrase "the Second Coming of Christ" never actually appears in the Bible. Whether or not the doctrine to which the phrase refers deserves rethinking, a popular abuse of it certainly needs to be named and rejected. If we believe that Jesus came in peace the first time, but that wasn't his "real" and decisive coming—it was just a kind of warm-up for the real thing—then we leave the door open to envisioning a second coming that will be characterized by violence, killing, domination, and eternal torture. . . . This eschatological understanding of a violent second coming leads us to believe (as we've said before) that in the end, even God finds it impossible to fix the world apart from violence and coercion; no one should be surprised when those shaped by this theology behave accordingly.

If we remain charmed by this kind of eschatology, we will be forced to see the nonviolence of the Jesus of the Gospels as a kind of strategic fake-out, like a feigned retreat in war, to be followed up by a crushing blow of so-called redemptive violence in the end. The gentle Jesus of the first coming becomes a kind of trick Jesus, a fake-me-out Messiah, to be replaced by the true jihadist Jesus of a violent second coming.

This is why I believe that many of our current eschatologies, intoxicated by dubious interpretations of John's Apocalypse, are not only ignorant and wrong, but dangerous and immoral.[9]

By referring to the "gentle Jesus" of the first coming, Brian McLaren misses the fact that Jesus came to die on the Cross to defeat sin (Mark 10:45), the devil, and death (Hebrews 2:14). These were all defeated by Jesus' sacrificial death on Calvary. As Jesus confronted hypocritical and wayward religious leaders, cast out demons, threw over the money-changers tables, and died on the Cross, it was much more than a "gentle" first coming. McLaren also misses the fact that when the Bible describes Jesus' return, it will not be as a "jihadist" terrorist returning but One who rightly judges those who have been in unholy rebellion against God and His Word (John 16:8).

McLaren is a perfect example of the Bible's warnings that "scoffers" will come in the last days—"mockers" with their ridiculing words about the Bible's description of the second coming of Jesus Christ:

Knowing this first, that there shall come in the last days scoffers, walking after their own lusts, And saying, Where is the promise of his coming? (2 Peter 3:3-4)

> But beloved, remember ye the words which were
> spoken before of the apostles of our Lord Jesus
> Christ; How that they told you there should be
> mockers in the last time, who should walk after
> their own ungodly lusts. These be they who
> separate themselves, sensual, having not the spirit.
> (Jude 17-19)

Brian McLaren and Rick Warren

It is quite apparent that Rick Warren and emerging church leaders like Brian McLaren are gradually moving into "spiritual formation" together. There are many other overlapping factors besides their almost identical statements to disregard prophecy. Warren uses the Schuller metaphor "God's Dream" to describe his P.E.A.C.E. Plan. McLaren suggests "God's Dream" as the first metaphor in the new spiritual language that he proposes the church adopt.[10] Warren told Ken Blanchard at a Lead Like Jesus conference—"You know, Ken, let's start a revolution.[11] And the second metaphor McLaren suggests for his new spiritual language is "revolution."[12] The similarities go on and on. In fact, McLaren attributes his becoming a pastor to Rick Warren. He writes:

> I first heard Rick share this material in 1985, when I
> was a college English professor. As I heard Rick share
> the story of Saddleback Valley Community Church,
> for the first time in my life I could envision a church
> that had authentic evangelism running through its
> veins, and for the first time I sensed that God might
> be inviting me to leave teaching to do this kind of
> church-based disciple-making. I literally would not
> be doing what I am doing if not for Rick's impact
> on my life.[13]

In his book *Everything Must Change*, Brian McLaren describes Rick Warren's Global P.E.A.C.E. Plan and is very supportive of it.[14] Both Warren and McLaren wrote personal forewords to emerging church leader Dan Kimball's book *The Emerging Church*. And they have also each worked with Evangelical leader Leonard Sweet. McLaren, who co-wrote a book with Sweet titled *A is for Abductive*, described Sweet as "brilliant":

> Without fail, when I am around this brilliant and contagiously thoughtful scholar and author, I think new thoughts in new ways.[15]

Leonard Sweet, though professing to be an Evangelical Christian, has embraced many influential New Age figures to the point of absorbing the essence of their teachings into his quantum spirituality.

Ten

Warren, Sweet, and Sweet's "New Light" Heroes

> Quantum spirituality bonds us to all creation as well as to other members of the human family. . . . This entails a radical doctrine of embodiment of God in the very substance of creation. . . . But a spirituality that is not in some way entheistic (whether pan- or trans-), that does not extend to the spirit-matter of the cosmos, is not Christian.[1]
>
> **—Leonard Sweet**

Shortly after *Deceived on Purpose* was published, I came across a book titled *Quantum Spirituality: A Postmodern Dialectic* written by Rick Warren's "Evangelical" colleague Leonard Sweet. Also, around the same time, I was given a cassette tape set of a presentation Sweet had done with Warren in 1995. Their recorded discussion is titled *The Tides of Change* and was packaged as part of an ongoing series called "Choice Voices for Church Leadership." At the time this audio project took place, Sweet was a Christian author, Methodist minister, and the Dean of the Theological School at Drew University. According to information on the tape set, this presentation was about ministry on the emerging "new frontier."[2]

Challenging pastors to make changes in their ministry to meet the emerging postmodern culture and the changing times, Sweet and Rick Warren present themselves not only as pastors but also as modern-day change agents. In their conversation together, Sweet enthusiastically remarked to Warren: "I think this is part of this New Spirituality that we are seeing birthed around us."[3]

In listening to this cassette-tape series, I found it interesting that Leonard Sweet was talking about the birth of a "New Spirituality" with Rick Warren way back in 1995. Since 9/11, "New Spirituality" is the term that most New Age leaders are now using instead of "New Age Spirituality." By simply removing the word "Age" from "New Age Spirituality," the "New Age Spirituality" has suddenly become the "New Spirituality." Emerging church figures like Sweet, Brian McLaren, and others are also employing the term "New Spirituality." They use it to describe the "new" Christianity they are practicing as "New Christians" and "New Light leaders."[4] What has become clear over the last decade is that the "New Spirituality"—with its bottom line belief that God is "in" everything—is, in reality, the foundational New Age "hub" for the coming New World Religion. This panentheistic New Age/New Spirituality teaching that God is "in" everything will be the "common ground" melting pot belief that the coming New World Religion will ultimately rest upon.

In *The Tides of Change*, it is clear that Rick Warren and Leonard Sweet are working toward a "New Reformation" of the church.[5] But as I read Sweet's book *Quantum Spirituality: A Postmodern Apologetic*, I quickly discovered that Sweet's New Reformation is really just a New Age re-formation of biblical Christianity—a New Spirituality. And his New Age/New Spirituality take on things is just one more reason to be concerned about the further New Age implications that are already so present in Warren's Purpose Driven movement.

Serving Two Masters

Although I was not previously familiar with Leonard Sweet, I knew that his book, *Quantum Spirituality*, had raised some concerns about his apparent affection for New Age teachings. When I began reading through *Quantum Spirituality*, I could see why people were concerned.

Highly intellectual and well-read, Leonard Sweet almost dares you to keep up with him as he charges through the spiritual marketplace. Operating at lightning speed and quoting from countless books and articles, he will impress many readers with his quick wit and spiritual insights. However, as he treacherously dives into New Age waters and challenges his readers to go there with him, serious problems arise within his "postmodern apologetic."

In reading *Quantum Spirituality*, I recalled the Sermon on the Mount when Jesus warned that you can't serve two masters (Matthew 6:24). Leonard Sweet may be a professing Evangelical Christian, but he also simultaneously praises New Age authors and their teachings. Observing Sweet's obvious New Age slant to Christianity, I was not surprised to see that he was one of the featured speakers at a 2007 leadership conference at the Crystal Cathedral.[6] He also co-led two small-group workshops with Warren in 2008.[7]

New Light Leaders?

While some Leonard Sweet defenders have argued that Sweet's hybridized postmodern "New Light" apologetic flies right over the heads of "old light" "fundamentalist" types, the facts tell a much different story. What I learned in reading *Quantum Spirituality* is that Sweet is in the process of trying to transform biblical Christianity into a quantum/postmodern/New Light/New Age/New Spirituality. Without apology, Sweet writes that he is part of a "New Light movement" and he describes those he especially admires as "New Light leaders."[8]

In the "Acknowledgments" of *Quantum Spirituality*, Sweet expresses his deep gratitude and admiration to various "New Light leaders" that he openly praises as "the most creative religious leaders in America today."[9] Included in his group are a number of New Age leaders I am very familiar with—most particularly Willis Harman, Matthew Fox, and M. Scott Peck. Sweet describes these three men—along with all the others cited—as "extraordinary" and "great" New Light leaders. He goes so far as to say that they are his "personal role models" and "heroes" of the "true nature of the postmodern apologetic." Sweet writes:

> They are my personal role models (in an earlier day one could get away with "heroes") of the true nature of the postmodern apologetic. More than anyone else, they have been my teachers on how to translate, without compromising content, the gospel into the indigenous context of the postmodern vernacular.[10]

But many of the men Leonard Sweet acknowledges have compromised the "content" of the Gospel by translating it into the "postmodern vernacular" of a New Age/New Spirituality. For example, Willis Harman, Matthew Fox, and M. Scott Peck have all played leading roles in the building and popularizing of today's New Age/New Spirituality movement. Therefore, how can these three leaders be Sweet's "role models" and "heroes"? Sweet's praise of these men says all you need to know about his "postmodern apologetic." Rather than commending these New Age/New Light leaders, a self-professing Christian leader like Sweet should be warning the church about them. A brief look at these three "New Light leaders" and their teachings will make this very clear.

Willis Harman

The late Willis Harman is one of Leonard Sweet's "personal role models" and "heroes," yet he is listed as one of the most influential Aquarian/New Age conspirators in the best-selling book *The Aquarian Conspiracy*, written by New Age proponent Marilyn Ferguson.[11] Her book was a 1980 trumpet blast announcing that the coming New Age—the Age of Aquarius—would eventually supplant biblical Christianity with its "heretical" New Age worldview that God is "in" everything. Ferguson writes:

Usually at the point of crisis, someone has a great
heretical idea. A powerful new insight explains
the apparent contradictions. It introduces a new
principle . . . a new perspective.[12]

For Harman's New Age influence to be identified in Ferguson's book speaks volumes about Harman. Ferguson believes in a
benevolent "Aquarian Conspiracy"—a conspiracy she taught would
eventually convert the world and the church to a postmodern
New Age worldview.

Willis Harman (1918-1997) was a social scientist/futurist with
the Stanford Research Institute where he started a futures research
program. Later he was President of the New Age Institute of No-
etic Sciences and was well connected to many New Age leaders.
Harman was very straightforward regarding his New Age beliefs.
He wrote a number of books including *Global Mind Change: The
New Age Revolution in How We Think.* In reviewing *Global Mind
Change,* The *San Francisco Chronicle* writes:

There never has been a more lucid interpretation of
New Age consciousness and what it promises for the
future than the works of Willis Harman.[13]

Yet in *Quantum Spirituality,* Leonard Sweet is drawn to Harman and his New Age views regarding the "Spiritual Sciences."
Sweet writes:

New Lights must catch the waves of a spiritual Gulf
Stream taking them into the unknown regions of
what Nobel laureate/philosopher/London School
of Economics professor Karl Popper and electrical
engineer/Stanford University professor Willis W.
Harman call the "Spiritual Sciences."[14]

In *Global Mind Change,* Willis Harman always defines "Spiritual Sciences" in conjunction with the "perennial wisdom" that

is the New Age and the occult. Harman states:

> The mystery of the creative/intuitive mind is underscored in the "perennial wisdom," which finds the deep intuition connected to the one Universal Mind. Thus there are indeed no limits to its capabilities save those the individual creates as part of the resistance to discovering one's godlike qualities.[15]

Unbelievably, a group of Evangelical leaders in the late 1970s was openly meeting with Willis Harman. These Christian leaders were exploring new and alternative views of the future. Disregarding the prophetic teachings of Scripture, they were looking for a different, more optimistic and hopeful view of the future than the one described in the Bible. Discernment Research Group reports:

> These Consultations on the Future represent the first publicly disclosed occasions where Evangelicals and New Agers met together to address common ground. Is it possible that this marked the beginning of the public phase of the integration of Theosophy [New Age/New Spirituality] with Christianity? Why did Evangelical leaders bring ... [New Age] Theosophist, Willis Harman, to address a 1979 Consultation on the topic of the future—when Scripture plainly teaches that our future blessed hope rests in Jesus Christ and His imminent return?[16]

In a 1995 journal article I wrote titled "Sign of the Times: Evangelicals and New Agers Together" and in *Reinventing Jesus Christ: The New Gospel* (2002), I describe how Christian leader Jay Gary was directly involved with the heavily New Age, former Assistant Secretary-General of the United Nations, Robert Muller. I warned that Gary was trying to subtly move the church into New Age teachings—particularly in regard to creating an alternative view of the future.[17] I had no idea then that Evangelical leaders had already met with New Age leaders in 1979 to try to find common ground and that these leaders were willing to disregard and manipulate the teachings of the Bible to create a different New Age view of the future. The beguiling illusion of "peace and safety" referred to in the Bible (1 Thessalonians 5:3) was obviously more attractive than the truth of biblical prophecy. Deceived Evangelical leaders like Leonard Sweet apparently felt they could gain more understanding from New Age leaders like Willis Harman than they could from a proper understanding of the Bible prophecy that Rick Warren and Brian McLaren were stating was none of our business.

Willis Harman's writings are greatly respected by a wide range of New Age leaders that includes veteran leader David Spangler. In his book, *Emergence: The Rebirth of the Sacred*, Spangler recommends Willis Harman's book *An Incomplete Guide to the Future*. He writes:

> This image of the new age is the one most popularly presented to the public, in books such as Willis Harman's *An Incomplete Guide to the Future*, Marilyn Ferguson's *The Aquarian Conspiracy*, and physicist Fritjof Capra's *The Turning Point*.[18]

Spangler also points out that Willis Harman was one of the leaders who helped to define how the New Age is emerging with "an increasingly clear set of ideas and values" that are defining a "new paradigm."[19] Yet in spite of Harman's well-publicized New Age credentials, Leonard Sweet praises Harman as his "role-model" and "hero."

Matthew Fox

Another one of Leonard Sweet's "personal role models" and "heroes" is Episcopalian priest Matthew Fox. Fox is a former Catholic priest who was excommunicated from the Catholic Church for openly professing the heretical teachings of Jesuit priest Pierre Teilhard de Chardin (and other New Age teachers). Chardin (1881-1955), who is frequently referred to as "the father of the New Age movement,"[20] believed that all of humanity is converging towards a universal New Age Christ in the future—an "Omega Point" that will forever change and redefine mankind.

Matthew Fox, like his mentor Chardin, taught that all creation is the "Cosmic Christ"—therefore the Cosmic Christ is in everyone and everything. In his book *The Coming of the Cosmic Christ*, Fox writes:

> We are all royal persons, creative, godly, divine, persons of beauty and of grace. We are all Cosmic Christs, "other Christs." But what good is this if we do not know it?[21]

> Divinity is found in all creatures. The divine name from Exodus 3:14, "I Am who I Am," is appropriated by Jesus who shows us how to embrace our own divinity. The Cosmic Christ is the "I am" in every creature. The divine mystery and miracle of existence is laid bare in the unique existence of each atom, each galaxy, each tree, bird, fish, dog, flower, star, rock, and human. Meister Eckhart says that "in this breakthrough I discover that God and I are one.[22]

Matthew Fox, in what he describes as "creation-centered spirituality," emphasizes that the Creator is "in" all "creation." Reflecting the all-embracing New Age philosophy of Pierre Teilhard de Chardin, Fox credits Chardin as one of the "key"[23] spokespersons for his creation-centered spirituality. In *Quantum Spirituality*, Leonard Sweet not only hails Matthew Fox as one of his spiritual "heroes," but he also describes Pierre Teilhard de Chardin—as "Twentieth-century Christianity's major voice."[24] Chardin's writings have never been officially recognized by the Catholic Church, but they have become increasingly popular over the years—not only with New

Agers but also with many Catholics and Catholic leaders.

Matthew Fox continues in the Chardin tradition. To his followers, Fox resembles the heroic, renegade priests in James Redfield's 1995 New Age best-seller, *The Celestine Prophecy*—the priests who dared to start a revolution by confronting the "Old Age" biblical theology with their New Age/New Spirituality insights. Like Chardin, Fox teaches original blessing rather than original sin and that Christ is panentheistic—a Cosmic Christ who is totally embedded in his creation. Fox quotes Pierre Teilhard de Chardin as saying that Christ is in even "the tiniest atom."[25]

In his 1988 book *The Coming of the Cosmic Christ*, Matthew Fox echoes Chardin's complaint that most people aren't interested in the concept of a "Cosmic Christ" that is "in" everything.[26] Today, however, it is a much different story as Fox and Chardin and their "Cosmic Christ" are being embraced by countless numbers of people, like Leonard Sweet, who describe themselves as Evangelical believers. In fact, Sweet betrays his own emerging New Age worldview by incorporating Fox's "Cosmic Christ" into his own book, *Quantum Spirituality*. Echoing Chardin, Fox, and many other New Age teachers today, Sweet writes:

> The world of nature has an identity and purpose apart from human benefit. But we constitute together a cosmic body of Christ [panentheism].[27]

Leonard Sweet actually credits Matthew Fox in a footnote for inspiring Sweet's own description of the "cosmic body of Christ"[28] and refers readers to Fox's book *The Coming of the Cosmic Christ* for more information on the subject.

In furthering his creation spirituality belief, Sweet writes:

> In an ecological model of the church, the earth is not separate from us; indeed, we are in symbiotic relationship with the earth. Creation spirituality is

of tremendous help here in weaning us from this homocentric warp.[29]

Leonard Sweet again credits Matthew Fox in a footnote that refers readers to more books written by Fox and by others regarding his Creation Spirituality Series:

> Books on creation spirituality include Matthew Fox, *Original Blessing: A Primer in Creation Spirituality Presented in Four Parts, Twenty-six Themes, and Two Questions* . . . Fox, *Creation Spirituality: Liberating Gifts for the Peoples of the Earth* . . . See also other volumes in the Creation Spirituality Series published by Bear and Company.[30]

Sweet then tries to differentiate what he is saying about creation spirituality from New Age pantheism (God "is" everything). To do so he presents Pierre Teilhard de Chardin and Matthew Fox's panentheism[31] (God is "in" everything). But Sweet doesn't explain that any kind of panentheism is still a distinctly heretical New Age teaching. Sweet crosses this panentheistic bridge into the New Age/New Spirituality right after his statement about the "cosmic body of Christ" and his footnotes to Matthew Fox. With characteristic assurance, Sweet lays bare his postmodern/quantum/New Age/New Spirituality "apologetic" by writing:

> Quantum spirituality bonds us to all creation as well as to other members of the human family. New Light pastors are what Arthur Peacocke calls "priests of creation"—earth ministers who can relate the realm of nature to God, who can help nurture a brother-sister relationship with the living organism called Planet Earth. This entails a radical doctrine of embodiment of God in the very substance of creation. *The Oxford Dictionary of the Christian Church* (1974) identifies the difference between pantheism and pan-entheism:

Pantheism is "the belief or theory that God and the universe are identical"; panentheism is "the belief that the Being of God includes and penetrates the whole universe, so that every part of it exists in Him, but . . . that His Being is more than, and is not exhausted by, the Universe." New Light spirituality does more than settle for the created order, as many forms of New Age pantheism do. *But a spirituality that is not in some way entheistic (whether pan- or trans-), that does not extend to the spirit-matter of the cosmos, is not Christian.* A quantum spirituality can in no way define God out of existence.[32] (emphasis added)

This panentheistic God "in" everything teaching by Leonard Sweet is the foundational teaching of the New Age/New Spirituality. But Sweet's emerging panentheistic New Spirituality agrees not only with the New Age but also with a Rick Warren statement in *The Purpose Driven Life*. As previously described, Warren uses a new, flawed translation of Ephesians 4:6 to present this same panentheistic/New Age teaching that God is "in" everything. Regarding God, Warren writes that the Bible says:

He rules everything and is everywhere and is in everything.[33] (*New Century Version*)

Because Rick Warren has never removed this improper translation from *The Purpose Driven Life*, he and Leonard Sweet appear to be on the same panentheistic/New Age page. The New Age implications of their writings relate directly to the following statement made by Pierre Teilhard de Chardin:

What I am proposing to do is to narrow that gap between pantheism and Christianity by bringing out what one might call the Christian soul of pantheism or the pantheist aspect of Christianity.[34]

In 2006, Matthew Fox published a book titled *A New Reformation: Christian Spirituality and the Transformation of Christianity*. Panentheism—God "in" everything—is the rallying cry for the New Age/New Reformation of Christianity that Matthew Fox and other New Age leaders are calling for. It is most significant that Leonard Sweet, Robert Schuller, Rick Warren, Brian McLaren, Erwin McManus, and other leading church figures are also calling for a New Reformation and transformation of Christianity as we know it. And while Warren has stated that his New Reformation is based on "deeds" not "creeds,"[35] the whole idea of a proposed New Reformation can be traced directly back to Schuller. In 1982, Schuller called for a New Reformation in his book *Self-Esteem: The New Reformation*. In 2003, Schuller further defined his New Reformation in panentheistic terms when he said that God was not only transcendent but "immanent." He stated, "Yes, God is alive and He is in every single human being!"[36] Meanwhile Warren has also been calling for a New Reformation[37] while citing a new version of the Bible that states that God is "in" everything.

M. Scott Peck

M. Scott Peck (1936-2005), the late psychiatrist and best-selling author of *The Road Less Traveled*, is another one of the "role models" and "heroes" that Leonard Sweet cites in his book *Quantum Spirituality*. *The Road Less Traveled* was on the *New York Times Best Seller* list for over ten years. In a sub-section of *The Road Less Traveled* titled "The Evolution of Consciousness," Peck describes God as being "intimately associated with us—so intimately that He is part of us."[38] He writes:

> If you want to know the closest place to look for grace, it is within yourself. If you desire wisdom greater than your own, you can find it inside you. . . . To put it plainly, our unconscious is God. God within us. We were part of God all the time.[39]

In a later book titled *The Different Drum*, M. Scott Peck makes it clear that while he saw himself as a "Christian," he believes that the salvation of the world lies in community—not so much in accepting and following Jesus Christ as one's Lord and Savior. He writes:

> In and through community lies the salvation of the world.
>
> Nothing is more important.
>
> [T]he human race today stands at the brink of self-annihilation. . . . I'm scared for my own skin. I'm even more scared for the skin of my children. And I'm scared for your skins. I want to save my skin. I need you, and you me, for salvation. We must come into community with each other. We need each other.[40]

But he then adds that certain rules will have to be changed:

> It is not impractical to consider seriously changing the rules of the game when the game is clearly killing you.[41]

Peck goes on to say that this changing of rules will also apply to the Christian church. Speaking to the church, he writes:

> If humankind is to survive, the matter of changing the rules is not optional.[42]

Of course, this is exactly what Jesus did not do—nor did His disciples. They died living by God's Word and God's rules rather than trying to change those rules to save their own "skin." In a 1995 journal article titled "M. Scott Peck: Community and the Cosmic Christ," I explain:

What Peck was advocating had serious implications for Christians who dared to put *their* Lord before the god of community. In language reminiscent of Alice Bailey, Peck emphatically states that "community is and must be inclusive. The great enemy of community is exclusivity. Groups that exclude others because they are poor or doubters or divorced or sinners or of some different race or nationality are not communities; they are cliques—actually defensive bastions against community."

What Peck seemed to be saying was, that to survive in the world we must be accommodating enough to form a world community in the interests of peace. Peck's definition of "Christian community" gives us an idea of just how accommodating the Christian faith ultimately will be. In his eyes *everyone* is a potential member of a "world" Christian community, no matter what their expressed faith might be. He says, " . . . any group of people (no matter what their religious persuasion or whether the word "Jesus" is ever spoken) who are willing to practice the love, discipline, and sacrifice that are required for the spirit of community, that Jesus extolled and exemplified, will be gathered together in his name and he will be there.[43]

Leonard Sweet describes himself as an Evangelical Christian, and yet at the same time has described M. Scott Peck as one of his "heroes?" The panentheistic New Age M. Scott Peck who said that God is within us and that we are part of God? A man who was willing to capitulate to the world rather than holding fast to biblical truth and to Jesus Christ as His Lord and Savior? Someone who would change the rules to save his own "skin"? Yet true heroes of the Christian faith uphold the Gospel in tough times—they don't abandon it. They have always been willing to die for what they believe, rather than change the rules to save their own "skin."

Peck and Fox Together

When Matthew Fox's *The Coming of the Cosmic Christ* was published in 1988—just two years after the release of M. Scott Peck's *The Different Drum*—the lead endorsement on the back cover of Fox's book was written by Peck. Peck writes:

> Fox's most daring, pioneering work yet, stimulating us to the kind of resurrection of values and practice required for planetary salvation.[44]

M. Scott Peck and Matthew Fox were obviously in New Age agreement. Peck, like Matthew Fox and Leonard Sweet, describes Pierre Teilhard de Chardin in glowing terms. Where Sweet describes Chardin as "Twentieth-century Christianity's major voice," Peck similarly describes Chardin as being perhaps "the greatest prophet of the evolutionary leap" to a New Paradigm—the supposed quantum leap that is moving mankind toward mystical, global consciousness and world community. Peck writes:

> [T]he number of people entering the mystical stage of development and transcending ordinary culture seems to have increased a thousandfold in the course of a mere generation or two . . . one wonders if the explosion in their numbers might represent a giant leap forward in the evolution of the human race, a leap toward not only mystical but global consciousness and world community. . . .
> Perhaps the greatest prophet of this leap was Teilhard de Chardin.[45]

And it is the mystical "Christ" of Willis Harman, Matthew Fox, M. Scott Peck, Pierre Teilhard de Chardin, and the New Age that challenges biblical Christianity today. Leonard Sweet reveals his New Age sympathies when he refers to Harman, Fox, and Peck as "extraordinary" New Light leaders. He further reveals his New Age affections when he describes Chardin as "Twentieth-century Christianity's major voice."[46] However, Chardin was *not* the major voice for twentieth-century Christianity, but he *was* the major voice for the New Age/New Spirituality that was seeking to re-form and overturn biblical Christianity. The following quotes from Chardin underscore his New Age worldview and belief in a universal New Age Christ. He writes:

> [T]he Cross still stands. . . .

> But this is on one condition, and one only: that it expand itself to the dimensions of a new age, and cease to present itself to us as primarily (or even exclusively) the sign of a victory over sin.[47]

> A general convergence of religions upon a universal Christ who fundamentally satisfies them all: that seems to me the only possible conversion of the world, and the only form in which a religion of the future can be conceived.[48]

> I believe that the Messiah whom we await, whom we all without any doubt await, is the universal Christ; that is to say, the Christ of evolution.[49]

It is no coincidence that New Age leader and popular *Chicken Soup for the Soul* co-author Jack Canfield uses a Pierre Teilhard de Chardin quote to preface the first story in his first *Chicken Soup for the Soul* book in 1993.[50] That Chardin quote is the same quote used by Bernie Siegel in his 1987 book *Love, Medicine & Miracles*[51] and by other New Age leaders like Marianne Williamson.[52] In Robert Schuller's 2005 book *Don't Throw Away Tomorrow: Living God's Dream For Your Life*, Schuller describes Pierre Teilhard de Chardin as "one of the most respected philosopher-theologians."[53] With both Leonard Sweet and Robert Schuller hailing the late New Age Chardin as a highly respected Christian voice, it is not surprising that Leonard Sweet has been a featured speaker at Schuller's Crystal Cathedral. Even given all of this, Sweet took his New Age involvement a step further. He actually sought the counsel of David Spangler, one of the most pronounced New Age leaders of our time.

Eleven

Sweet, Spangler, and Quantum Spirituality

If we want to possess a magical crystal for our New Age work, we need look no further than our own bodies and the cells that make them up.[1]

—**David Spangler 1991**

I am grateful to David Spangler for his help in formulating this "new cell" understanding of New Light leadership.[2]

—**Leonard Sweet 1991**

Leonard Sweet, in acknowledging Willis Harman, Matthew Fox, M. Scott Peck, and the others he refers to as "New Light leaders" in *Quantum Spirituality*, states:

> I believe these are among the most creative religious leaders in America today. These are the ones carving out channels for new ideas to flow. In a way this book was written to guide myself through their channels and chart their progress. The book's best ideas come from them.[3]

Speaking of spiritual "channels," Sweet expresses his personal gratitude in *Quantum Spirituality* to channeler and veteran New Age leader, David Spangler. Spangler, in attempting to cast off the negative stereotype of a New Age *channeler*, would now more likely describe himself as a *conscious intuitive*.[4] A pioneering spokesperson for the New Age, Spangler has written numerous books over the years that include *Emergence: The Rebirth of the Sacred, Revelation: The Birth of a New Age,* and *Reimagination of the World: A Critique of the New Age, Science, and Popular Culture.* His book *Revelation: The Birth of a New Age* is a compilation of channeled transmissions he received from his disembodied spirit-guide "John." At one point in *Revelation,* Spangler documents what "John" prophesied about "the energies of the Cosmic Christ" and "Oneness":

> As the energies of the Cosmic Christ become increasingly manifest within the etheric life of Earth, many individuals will begin to respond with the realization that the Christ dwells within them. They will feel his presence moving within and through them and will begin to awaken to their heritage of Christhood and Oneness with God, the Beloved.[5]

Unbelievably, in a modern-day consultation that bears more than a casual resemblance to King Saul's consultation with the witch of Endor (1 Samuel 28:7), Leonard Sweet acknowledges in *Quantum Spirituality* that he was privately corresponding with channeler David Spangler.[6] In *Quantum Spirituality,* Sweet writes about what he calls his "new cell" understanding of New Light leadership, then closes his book by thanking Spangler for "his help in formulating this 'new cell' understanding of New Light Leadership." Sweet writes:

> Philosopher Eric Voegelin's word "cosmion" refers to "a well ordered thing that has the character of the universe." New Lights offer up themselves as the cosmions of a mind-of-Christ consciousness. As a cosmion incarnating the cells of a new body, New Lights will function as transitional vessels through which transforming energy can renew the divine image in the world, moving postmoderns from one state of embodiment to another.[7]

I am grateful to David Spangler for his help in formulating this "new cell" understanding of New Light leadership.[8]

Spangler: Still the New Age

In David Spangler's 1991 book, *The Reimagination of the World*, Spangler makes it clear that any "new cell" understanding associated with him is directly related to New Age teachings. While Spangler tries to distance himself from the more narcissistic and superficial aspects of the New Age, he still holds firm to the use of the term "New Age" to describe his spiritual beliefs. In fact, in referring to the importance of a "new cell understanding" of the New Age, Spangler writes:

> To me, a more appropriate symbol for the New Age is the cell. The cell is really a living crystal. It possesses a highly structured internal order, yet this geometry is organized around information rather than around position, as in a crystal lattice. Protoplasm is highly dynamic; it can give birth to endless varieties of new life, yet it can also collect and focus energy in powerful ways. If we want to possess a magical crystal for our New Age work, we need look no further than our own bodies and the cells that make them up.[9]

Was all of this part of the "new cell" understanding that Leonard Sweet received from David Spangler? This paragraph alone—much less Spangler's well documented "New Age work" through the years—should be enough to drive any Christian leader far away from Spangler's heretical New Age teachings. Sweet's involvement with a key New Age leader and channeler of spirit-guides is not innovative or edgy or pioneering—it is spiritually dangerous. The Bible instructs us to reprove and expose the works of darkness—not join forces with them (Ephesians 5:11-13).

Leonard Sweet's *Quantum Spirituality* and David Spangler's *The Reimagination of the World* were both published in 1991. It seems obvious from their books that both men are attempting to distance themselves from the more faddish, consumer-oriented elements of the New Age—but without actually dispensing with the term New Age itself.[10] To the casual reader, it might look like Spangler and Sweet are actually speaking *against* the New Age. In fact, quotes taken out of context might even make it appear this is true. But this is definitely not the case. Sweet and Spangler are just doing some New Age/New Spirituality public relations. They are both redefining and refining the term New Age as they try to strip the term of its Shirley MacClainesque pop aspects and put it more in the realm of seemingly authoritative science. The term New Age would no longer be associated with occult spiritual beliefs but rather with a period of time—a new era—in which their seemingly scientifically based spiritual beliefs would manifest. It would no longer be a New Age Spirituality. It would now be a universal "New Spirituality" for a new era—the coming "New Age." This New Age would be equated with a planetary era and a planetary ethic that would reflect a passionate concern for the environment and all of humanity. This new era would also reflect the new "civility" called for by Sweet's "hero," the late New Age leader M. Scott Peck. In his 1993 book *A World Waiting to be Born: Civility Rediscovered*, Peck writes the following about his Utopian New Age:

> The distinguishing feature of the citizens of Utopia is not their location, nationality, religion, or occupation but their commitment to becoming ever more civil individuals and their membership in a planetary culture of civility. By virtue of this commitment and membership, regardless of their theology, they welcome the active presence of God into both their individual and their collective lives. . . . Although their primary allegiance is to the

development of their own souls, they are all involved
in teaching as well as learning civility and dedicated
to inviting others into their planetary culture.[11]

Who is going to argue with this call for ecological responsibility, human compassion, and planetary "civility" in this coming
New Era—in this idealized New Age? Only those who recognize
that New Age beliefs are being smuggled in under the cover of a
new planetary ethic—a New Spirituality and a New Worldview for
the coming New Age. Leonard Sweet and Brian McLaren would
also try to redefine the term New Age more as a period of time
than as a set of occult beliefs. Attempting to marginalize the whole
New Age movement by characterizing it as "vague, consumerist,
undefined, and mushy," McLaren misses the fact that the New Age
is a well-organized spiritual movement with a long-standing hostility
to biblical Christianity. The New Age is very serious about what
it believes and is anything but "mushy." But as McLaren wrongly
defines the New Age as "mushy" while simultaneously equating
biblical Christianity with "pushy fundamentalism," he paves the
way for a newly emerging theology—a New Spirituality for a New
Age. The term "New Age" that characterized an occult belief system neatly disappears as the "New Age" simply becomes the time
frame in which this New Spirituality appears. In his book *Finding
our Way Again*, McLaren describes this New Spirituality for the
coming "New Age":

> The word *spirituality* tries to capture that fusion of
> everyday sacredness. For many people, it represents
> a life-giving alternative to secularist fundamentalism
> and religious fundamentalism, the former offering
> the world weapons of mass destruction and the latter
> stirring emotions to put the suicidal machinery into
> motion.
>
> This dissatisfaction in some cases has led to a
> reactionary resurgence of pushy fundamentalism—

fearful, manic, violent, apocalyptic. And in other cases it has led to a search for a new kind of spirituality. The success or failure of this search will, no doubt, play a major role in the story of the twenty-first century.

In its early stages, this search for spirituality has been associated with the term *new age*, which for many means something vague, consumerist, undefined, and mushy. However, in the aftermath of September 11, 2001, more and more of us are realizing that a warm but mushy spirituality is no match for hot and pushy fundamentalism, of whatever religious variety . . . More and more of us feel, more and more intensely, the need for a fresh, creative alternative—a fourth alternative, something beyond militarist scientific secularism, pushy religious fundamentalism, and mushy amorphous spirituality.

This alternative, we realize, needs to be creative and new to face the new challenges of a new age, a world gone "post-al"—postmodern, postcolonial, post-Enlightenment, post-Christendom, post-Holocaust, post-9/11. Yet it also needs to derive strength from the old religious traditions; it needs to face new-age challenges with age-old wisdom.[12]

Thus, the new semantics introduced by both New Age and Christian leaders—what had been called New Age Spirituality—would now be a panentheistic New Spirituality for a New Era and a New Age. Leonard Sweet, Brian McLaren, and other Christian leaders were slowly transitioning the church into New Age teachings, but with clever new terms like New Light leadership, quantum spirituality, New Spirituality and a New Worldview that will—for the "good of the world"—transition the church out of an "Old Age"/biblical Christianity into the emerging "New Age" of a New Spirituality.

In 1991, Leonard Sweet was setting the stage for everything

happening in the church today. He was saying what McLaren is now saying. He was starting to redefine the New Age as a New Era rather than a set of occult beliefs. In *Quantum Spirituality*, he writes:

> The church stands on the front lines of the coming reign of God. Or as biblical scholar J. Christiaan Beker entitles his chapter on Paul's ecclesial thought, "The Church [is] the Dawning of the New Age." The event of Jesus Christ spells the end of the old age and the beginning of the new age. The church then is the "beachhead of the new creation," in Beker's words, "the sign of the new age in the old world that is 'passing away.'"[13]

Thus while David Spangler, Brian McLaren, and Leonard Sweet all seem to be distancing themselves from the New Age—they are actually helping to bring it on. They are bringing it on because they hold to the basic New Age view that we are all "one" because God is "in" everything, as Sweet shares in *Quantum Spirituality*. To underline this idea, Sweet turns to contemplative mystic/panentheist Thomas Merton. Sweet states:

> If the church is to dance, however, it must first get its flabby self back into shape. . . . So far the church has refused to dip its toe into postmodern culture. A quantum spirituality challenges the church to bear its past and to dare its future by sticking its big TOE into the time and place of the present.
>
> Then, and only then, will a flattened out, "one-dimensional," and at times dimensionless world have discovered the power and vitality of a four-dimensional faith . . . Then and only then, will a New Light movement of "world-making" faith have helped to create the world that is to, and may yet, be. Then, and only then, will earthlings have uncovered

the meaning of these words, some of the last words poet/activist/contemplative/bridge between East and West Thomas Merton uttered: "We are already one. But we imagine that we are not. And what we have to recover is our original unity."[14]

Repackaging the New Age

So while TV psychics, crystal-mania, and Shirley MacLaine caricatures are contrasted to David Spangler and Leonard Sweet's revised definition of the New Age, the panentheistic doctrine that "we are all one" because Christ is "in" everything remains completely intact. Thus, nothing has really changed. The New Age with its quantum/universal/Cosmic Christ is still the same heretical spirituality with the same heretical New Age "Christ." The New Age has just been repackaged for an unsuspecting world and a very undiscerning church. In *The Reimagination of the World*, Spangler writes:

> Where is the Christ that is revealing itself and incarnating now? Where is the Christ in nature and in the Earth? Where is the feminine Christ?[15]

> With new discoveries in biology and quantum physics, we are seeing more and more what mystics have always seen: the process side of reality, its interconnectedness, its interpenetratingness, its blendedness. Where is the Christ in this expanding worldview?

> The Christ becomes the Cosmic Christ. Just as an advertiser can repackage a product and call it "new and improved," so the Cosmic Christ repackages the Christ. In fact, the essential qualities of this presence remain the same. The Christ is the Christ is the Christ. That is true whether we view its actions within an individual, a planet, or the cosmos as a whole. However, the new packaging may make it

more accessible to people and help us to recognize some of those qualities of the Christ that we have been overlooking for the past two thousand years.[16]

Obviously, Leonard Sweet is doing his own "new packaging" as he refers to New Age leaders like Willis Harman, Matthew Fox, and M. Scott Peck as "New Light leaders." But their "Cosmic Christ" is the false Christ of the New Age/New Spirituality. Their "Cosmic Christ" is not the Bible's Jesus Christ, but a false Christ of which the real Jesus Christ warns us to beware. Spangler leaves no room for doubt in describing this New Age "Cosmic Christ" not as a "he" but rather as an "it":

> Therefore, the Cosmic Christ is the Christ that is freed from a particular historical event. It is active throughout the whole range of time. It is active in each of us, whether we are Christians or not, and it holds the promise that we can each be incarnations of the sacred. It reveals its feminine side and the side that is beyond gender. It is present within nature. It is the spirit of sacredness within the Earth and within the whole cosmos. It is as present in other faith traditions, including many of those we call pagan, as it is in Christianity, and sometimes it seems to me that it is more present in other religious understandings than in some of the Christian denominations whose attitudes and actions betray the compassionate, universal, and loving qualities of the Christ.[17]

Why would Leonard Sweet consult with a New Age leader like David Spangler and then write favorably about a panentheistic Cosmic Christ who is "in" everyone and everything? Sweet underscores this when he writes:

> The world of nature has an identity and purpose apart from human benefit. But we constitute together a cosmic body of Christ.[18]

In *Quantum Spirituality*, it is clear that even with all of Leonard Sweet's postmodern vernacular and Evangelical language, he is still a New Age sympathizer to the nth degree. Sweet's affection for New Age teachers and for the Cosmic Christ is right in his book *Quantum Spirituality*, posted in its entirety on his website, as of this writing, for all to see. One church poll describes Sweet as one of the most influential Christian leaders today,[19] but the late Aquarian Conspiracy author Marilyn Ferguson would have identified someone with his beliefs as a fellow Aquarian Conspirator.

Leonard Sweet and Rick Warren

Leonard Sweet's book *Quantum Spirituality* clearly reveals the New Age implications of Sweet's "double-tongued" (1 Timothy 3:8) and double-minded" (James 1:8) teachings. Yet the New Age implications of Sweet's ministry do not carry over to Rick Warren based on one talk they gave together in 1995; however, there is more to this than *The Tides of Change* joint presentation. Warren further aligns himself with this New Age sympathizer when he endorsed Sweet's 1999 book *SoulTsunami: Sink or Swim in New Millennium Culture*. Warren's endorsement was not only featured on the book's front and back covers, but was actually incorporated into the front cover design.[20] Warren's endorsement obviously gives Sweet and his book added credibility. By openly endorsing Sweet's book, the further New Age implications of Warren's ministry were becoming even more apparent. Not surprisingly, in *SoulTsunami* Sweet quickly introduces the Robert Schuller/Rick Warren/New Age/emerging church themes of "God's Dream" for the world and a "New Reformation" for the church. He writes:

> The time to save God's Dream is now. The people to save God's Dream are you . . . .

> God is birthing the greatest spiritual awakening

in the history of the church. God is calling you to
midwife that birth. Are you going to show up?[21]

While the world is rethinking its entire cultural
formation, it is time to find new ways of being the
church that are true to our postmodern context. It
is time for a Postmodern Reformation.[22]

But Leonard Sweet is the one who is dreaming. God is not
birthing the greatest spiritual awakening in the history of the
church. Quite the contrary. It is the New Age/New Spirituality that has been growing exponentially over the years and is
reaching a crescendo as New Age books and teachings are everywhere—including in the church. Oprah Winfrey and other New
Age spokespeople are also talking about a great "awakening"
and about "God's Dream," but their "awakening" is to the false
Christ—the Cosmic Christ—not to Jesus Christ as their Lord and
Savior. Christian leaders like Leonard Sweet and Rick Warren
are making no differentiation between the church and the New
Age/New Spirituality.

With regard to a "Postmodern Reformation" of the church,
Matthew Fox published *his* call for a New Age/New Reformation
of the church in his 2006 book *A New Reformation: Creation
Spirituality and the Transformation of Christianity*. Fox's New Reformation is based on the panentheistic New Age/New Spirituality
teaching that "All things are in God and God is in all things."[23]
Are we to believe that Leonard Sweet and his "hero" Matthew
Fox are not talking about the same New Postmodern Reformation of the church?

Rick Warren's working relationship with Leonard Sweet was
further underlined when he and Sweet co-led two highly publicized small-group workshops in 2008 that were held in Atlanta,
Georgia and at Warren's Saddleback Church.[24] The Saddleback
small-group workshop with Warren and Sweet was called Wired,
and the theme of the gathering was "Prepare your church for

spiritual growth and connectivity."[25] Commenting on small groups in his book *Quantum Spirituality*, Sweet sounds just like Matthew Fox when he writes the following:

> The power of small groups is in their ability to develop the discipline to get people "in-phase" with the *Christ consciousness* and *connected* with one another. [26] (emphasis added)

My former New Age teachers couldn't have said it any better. "Christ-consciousnes" is a popular New Age term that has been used by channelers, gurus, shamans, psychics, and practitioners of the occult for years. The big question for Leonard Sweet—and for Rick Warren—is what "Christ" are you getting "connected" to in these small groups? What "Christ consciousness" are you getting "in-phase" with? The apostle Paul warns about confusing the body of Christ with the body of a harlot or false Christ:

> Know ye not that your bodies are the members of Christ? shall I then take the members of Christ, and make them members of an harlot? God forbid. What? know ye not that he which is joined to an harlot is one body? for two, saith he, shall be one flesh. (1 Corinthians 6:15-16)

In yet another place Paul warns:

> I marvel that ye are so soon removed from him that called you into the grace of Christ unto another gospel: Which is not another; but there be some that trouble you, and would pervert the gospel of Christ. But though we, or an angel from heaven, preach any other gospel unto you than that which we preached unto you, let him be accursed. (Galatians 1:6-7)

"As Christian As Anyone Can Get"

Given all of Leonard Sweet's New Age/New Spirituality sympathies, Rick Warren has continued to work with Sweet and promote him rather than separate himself from him and expose him as the Bible admonishes him to do:

> And have no fellowship with the unfruitful works of darkness, but rather reprove them. (Ephesians 5:11)

There is an interesting twist here. Richard Abanes—Rick Warren's most outspoken apologist and someone who has written extensively on the New Age—actually wrote an article defending Leonard Sweet and Warren's involvement with him. In a 2008 article titled "Leonard Sweet, Rick Warren and the New Age," Abanes writes:

> Doctrinally/theologically, Leonard Sweet is about as Christian as anyone can get.[27]

Unbelievable! The man who consults with New Age leader David Spangler and describes Willis Harman, Matthew Fox, and M. Scott Peck as his "personal role models" and "heroes" is "about as Christian as anyone can get?" Perhaps Abanes has forgotten what he once wrote about Peck and Spangler in his 1995 book *The Less Traveled Road and the Bible: A Scriptural Critique of the Philosophy of M. Scott Peck*. In this book that Abanes co-wrote with H. Wayne House, in a section written by Abanes, he writes very forthrightly about Peck's and Spangler's involvement in the New Age movement. Describing both Peck and Spangler as "New Agers" and warning about their promotion of the New Age concept of "oneness," Abanes writes:

> Peck is echoing a concept found in Hinduism and Buddhism, namely, that all reality is oneness and that

> what we perceive to be individuality is an illusion . . . .
> The above concept is a major tenet of the New
> Age movement, as New Age spokesperson David
> Spangler demonstrates when he writes, "Oneness
> is a key concept. In a spiritual sense, the world has
> always been one. . . ."

> Like all New Agers, Peck embraces the belief that
> realization of our oneness with God—or our own
> godhood—is essential to spiritual growth and
> freedom from problems. Attaining godhood is really
> the only reason we exist. Realization of our divinity
> is also the whole purpose behind evolution, which
> is another "miracle" to Peck.[28]

Given these strong warnings, why is Richard Abanes now
defending Leonard Sweet from those who are concerned about
Sweet's enchantment with the same M. Scott Peck and David
Spangler that Abanes had previously exposed as New Agers?
Rather than taking Sweet to task for aligning himself with New
Agers like Peck and Spangler, Abanes takes Sweet's critics to
task. Almost inexplicably, Abanes admonishes Sweet's critics for
suggesting there are New Age implications not only to Sweet's
teachings but also to Rick Warren's involvement with Sweet.
This seems to contradict his own past writings about Peck,
Spangler, and the New Age.

As an apologist for Rick Warren, Abanes obviously wishes
to protect Warren. But in this case he is hurting him more than
helping him. In refusing to acknowledge the New Age implications of Warren's involvement with a New Age sympathizer like
Leonard Sweet, Abanes does a great disservice to the body of
Christ—and to Rick Warren himself.

One final note of irony in regard to Richard Abanes, Leonard
Sweet, M. Scott Peck, and the New Age. In the introduction to
his 1995 book about M. Scott Peck, Abanes actually quoted from
the journal article I had written about Peck earlier that same

year. In my article, which was titled "M. Scott Peck: Community and the Cosmic Christ," I described how Peck had initiated a spiritual "revolution" that was attempting to redefine biblical Christianity with deceptive New Age teachings that came in the name of Christ. Recognizing the validity of my warnings about Peck and the New Age, Abanes opened his book by favorably quoting me. He wrote:

> Christian author Warren Smith notes in a 1995 article for the *SCP Journal* that Peck single-handedly "helped to spark a spiritual revolution that is still going on today." Peck's influence on the Christian church has been especially strong since his alleged conversion in 1980 to Christianity. Smith explains:
>
> "His [Peck's] writings over the last decade or so have also caused Christians to reexamine their faith in light of his teachings. His books are often found in Christian bookstores. There is no question that his writings and his endorsements of others have had a profound impact on the spiritual marketplace."[29]

Doesn't Richard Abanes see that the statement he quoted from my article back then is just as applicable today? That this same deceptive "spiritual revolution" is still going on? Only now, M. Scott Peck's "spiritual revolution" is coming even more directly from within the church through New Age sympathizers like Leonard Sweet and others.

What Revolution?

The "spiritual revolution" I referenced in my 1995 journal article and that Richard Abanes cites in his book about M. Scott Peck, is indeed the same New Age "revolution" attempting to transfix and transform the church today. We should be very concerned when self-professing Evangelical leaders with New Age sympathies talk about starting a "spiritual revolution."

In chapter four, I described how New Age sympathizer Ken Blanchard recounted at a 2003 Lead Like Jesus conference that Rick Warren had turned to him and stated: "You know, Ken, let's start a revolution."[30] Five years later Blanchard was calling his Lead Like Jesus conference a Lead Like Jesus "Revolution."[31] In his book *The Secret Message of Jesus*, Brian McLaren's second suggested metaphor after "God's Dream" is "revolution of God."[32] And McLaren's book *Everything Must Change* is even subtitled *Jesus, Global Crises, and a Revolution of Hope.* Erwin McManus, another emerging church leader, calls for an "Evolution of a Revolution" in his Rick Warren endorsed book *The Unstoppable Force.*[33] It is noteworthy that New Age leader Neale Donald Walsch has also talked of an "evolution revolution"[34] that will be an "unstoppable force."[35] *Organized* Christianity and the New Age are overlapping and blending so much that soon—very soon—there will be no distinguishing the two as they blend right into the New Spirituality of the New World Religion.

Overlapping terms like "revolution," "reformation," "as above, so below," "God's Dream," "Cosmic Christ," "Oneness," and "God in everything" are being used to transition what was once considered traditional Christianity into the New Spirituality of a New Age. New Age leader Marianne Williamson has stated that the New Age/New Spirituality "revolution" is "a global phenomenon that will change the cellular structure of the human race." In her 2004 book *The Gift of Change*, she writes:

> An underground revolution is sweeping the hearts and minds of the people of the world, and it is happening despite the wars and terror that confront us. This revolution is a fundamental change of worldview, and it carries with it the potential to reorganize the structure of human civilization. It brings a basic shift in the thoughts that dominate the world. It wages a peace that will end all war. It is

a global phenomenon that will change the cellular structure of the human race.[36]

An underground "revolution" that will be a "global phenomenon" bringing peace to the world? A "revolution" that will "change the cellular structure of the human race"? David Spangler describes the cell as the basic metaphor of the New Age, while Leonard Sweet thanks Spangler for helping him to formulate the "new cell theory" of his quantum spirituality. In the meantime, Rick Warren and Brian McLaren describe a spiritual "revolution" that could change history[37] and change everything.[38] New Age leaders Marianne Williamson and Neale Donald Walsch also talk of a spiritual "revolution" that could change history and "change everything."[39]

On the surface, this talk of a revolutionary world peace that will change everything sounds admirable. However, this "peace" is based on deceptive New Age principles, not on a sound biblical foundation. Christian leaders seem to be taking the church—into a quantum spirituality of a New Age/New Spirituality—into a New Worldview—into the coming New World Religion.

Whose Revolution?

"The Evolution of a Revolution"
>—**Erwin McManus**, *Unstoppable Force* (p. 102)

"If you ever get a chance to hang out with Mack, you will soon learn that he's hoping for a revolution."
>—**William Paul Young**, *The Shack* (p. 248)

"The time has come for a new kind of conversation, a new kind of Christianity, a new kind of revolution."
>—**Shane Claiborne**, *Irresistible Revolution* (p. 29)

"An underground revolution is sweeping the hearts and minds of the people of the world. . . . This revolution is a fundamental change of worldview."
>—**Marianne Williamson**, *The Gift of Change*, (p. 279)

"The world is undergoing an extraordinary revolution, an intellectual rebellion against the exclusionary belief structure that has dominated Western thought for centuries."
>—**Willis Harman**, *The Global Mind Change*, back cover

"The translucent revolution is about human consciousness and could lay the foundation for an evolutionary leap in human life unlike anything we have known."
>—**Barbara Marx Hubbard**, *Translucent Revolution* (p. 419)

"[I]gniting a revolution of hope that can change everything. Beginning with you. Beginning now."
>—**Brian McLaren**, *Everything Must Change*, back cover

"You know, Ken, let's start a revolution."
>—**Rick Warren to Ken Blanchard**
Lead Like Jesus Conference, Birmingham, Alabama, 2003

Twelve

Fractals, Chaos Theory, Quantum Spirituality, and *The Shack*

A fractal . . . something considered simple and orderly that is actually composed of repeated patterns no matter how magnified. A fractal is almost infinitely complex. I love fractals, so I put them everywhere.[1]

—Sarayu, *The Shack*

Fractals reveal a hidden "order" underlying all seemingly chaotic events. The fractals are intricate and beautiful. They repeat basic patterns, but with an infinity of variations and forms. The world-view emerging from this scientific research is new, and yet at the same time very very ancient.[2]

—The Sovereign Court and
Order of the Ancient Dragon

Shortly after writing the previous two chapters on Leonard Sweet and quantum spirituality, I spoke at a church in Southern California. I had been asked to speak at the two morning services and then again in the evening. In the second morning service, three women approached me and thanked me for warning about the New Age/New Spirituality and how it was working its way into the church. All three told me they formerly attended Rick Warren's Saddleback Church, but they had become dissatisfied and left. They said it had been difficult to leave because so many of their friends still went to Saddleback.

After the evening service, two more women approached me with similar stories. One left Saddleback the previous year and the other had left a church she had been attending for over thirty-seven years. This second woman, Jennifer, had left because her former church was introducing a mixture of Purpose Driven, church growth, and emerging church teachings. She was following up on comments I made about William Paul Young's *New York Times* best-selling book *The Shack*. I had described how *The Shack's* author had introduced New Age concepts into his emotional novel about a man's supposed encounter with "God," "Jesus," and the "Holy Spirit" after the brutal murder of his daughter. In the midst of his story, Young suddenly introduces the foundational teaching of the New Age/New Spirituality/New World Religion–that God is "in" everything. *The Shack's* "Jesus" told Mack–the distraught father and main character in the novel–that God is "in" all things:

> God, who is the ground of all being, dwells in, around, and through all things.[3]

In speaking to the Southern California church, I had explained that the Bible makes it clear that God is not "in" all things. I explained that Satan–"the god of this world"–wants everyone to believe that God is "in" all things because then everyone would have reason to believe that they were God. When *The Shack's* "Jesus" states that God is "in" all things, he actually reinforces what Rick Warren has already written in *The Purpose Driven Life*–that the Bible says God is "in" everything.[4] In an online article I wrote titled "*The Shack* and its New Age Leaven," I discuss this "God in everything" aspect.[5]

In our brief conversation, the second woman, Jennifer, told me she had discovered something interesting in *The Shack* and had written a short article about it. She asked if I would be willing to read her article. I told her I would.

Fractal Theory and *The Shack*

Back home a week later, I found Jennifer's paper in my notebook. I was intrigued by the title—"Fractal Theory in *The Shack*." In her article, Jennifer explains that during her research she had rented a DVD movie, which she had been told had New Age undertones. She then describes something she discovered in the movie:

> In the movie *The Seeker* a young boy is a chosen one who is to find signs hidden throughout time, which will help fight against the encroaching darkness. I won't go into the plot too much but what I will say is, in the movie, each sign that the boy is to find is known as a fractal. When I heard the term fractal, right away I realized that I had heard that same term somewhere else recently. Later on that day I remembered where I had heard it, *The Shack.*
>
> Beginning in chapter 9 in *The Shack* which is titled, "A Long Time Ago in a Garden Far, Far Away," we read about how Sarayu (who represents the Holy Spirit) has created a garden and we learn that the garden is a fractal. We learn about fractals from Sarayu when she says, "A fractal is something considered simple and orderly that is actually composed of repeated patterns no matter how magnified. A fractal is almost infinitely complex. I love fractals, so I put them everywhere."[6]

Curious about the term "fractal" that was showing up in both *The Shack* and *The Seeker*, Jennifer did some research. What she discovered is that the term "fractal" is directly related to what are being called the "new sciences" of "Chaos Theory" and "Fractal Theory." What was of particular interest to me was her finding that fractals are directly linked with the occult phrase "as above, so below"—the same occult/New Age term that Eugene Peterson had mysteriously inserted into his paraphrase of the Lord's

Prayer. And now, here was Peterson's endorsement prominently featured on the front cover of *The Shack*. Given my previously expressed concern about Peterson's use of "as above, so below" in *The Message*, I found it interesting that "as above, so below" was apparently related to the term fractal in *The Shack* and that Peterson had so enthusiastically endorsed the book.

As Above, So Below and Fractals

After reading Jennifer's article, I made sure a copy was sent to the Indiana pastor who had sent me the articles regarding Norman Vincent Peale. Because he had been currently writing articles exposing *The Shack's* errant theology, I knew he would be interested in Jennifer's article—how she had discovered a direct link between *The Shack's* multiple references to fractals and the New Age term "as above, so below."[7]

Later, as we talked by phone, the pastor searched the Internet for the word "fractal." The first website listed was called "Fractal Wisdom." The site featured an article titled "Fractal Chaos Crashes the Wall between Science and Religion."[8] Under that heading was a box containing a fractal design, and underneath the fractal was the saying "As Above, So Below." Underneath the occult saying was a quote from New Age pioneer and mystic Aldous Huxley—the single most quoted person in Marilyn Ferguson's best-selling New Age book *The Aquarian Conspiracy*. Huxley is also quoted by Rick Warren in *The Purpose Driven Life*.[9] Huxley's quote on the Fractal Wisdom website addresses the dual subjects of chaos and "purpose":

> At any given moment, life is completely senseless.
> But viewed over a period, it seems to reveal itself
> as an organism existing in time, having a purpose,
> trending in a certain direction.[10]

The online article titled "Fractal Chaos Crashes the Wall Between Science and Religion" goes on to state:

> New discoveries in the science and mathematics of
> Chaos research are revolutionizing our world view.
> They reveal a hidden fractal order underlying all
> seemingly chaotic events. The fractals are intricate
> and beautiful. They repeat basic patterns, but with
> an infinity of variations and forms. The world-view
> emerging from this scientific research is new, and yet
> at the same time ancient. With a little thought, and
> the help of this web, you can better understand the
> significance of Chaos and Fractals. You can see how
> to use these insights in your life to create a bridge
> between Science and Spirituality.[11]

> As the mystic sages of long ago put it, "as above, so
> below."[12]

But what is being presented as "science" is actually an occult/
New Age worldview, which presents the New Age belief that much
of the "chaos" in the world is the result of people not properly
perceiving the "interconnectedness" of all things. In other words,
what appears to be "chaos" is often just "the observer" not seeing
the "as above, so below"/God "in" everything/"fractal order"
that defines all creation. This postulated fractal order is directly
related to Teilhard de Chardin, Matthew Fox, and Leonard Sweet's
quantum spirituality/Creation Spirituality. *The Shack's* references
to fractals—references I had overlooked when I first read the
book—immediately explain why author William Young capitalizes
the letter "C" in the word "Creation" at least twenty times in *The
Shack*. The capital "C" reflects what his "Jesus" is teaching—that
God is "in" all things—including "Creation."

From the perspective of the New Age/New Spirituality, it
makes perfect sense that *The Shack's* "Jesus" states that God is
"in" all things. Mack—the main character—is seeing his life as "a
mess" rather than as a "fractal" part of "God." This is because he
is not seeing the "as above, so below" fractal order of "God in all
things." From this perspective, it also makes perfect sense that *The*

Shack's "Holy Spirit" told Mack that his life only seems chaotic and "a mess"—that in reality, he was actually "a living fractal."[13]

From this "Fractal Wisdom" website, I could see the deceptive New Age ploy regarding the word fractal and its relationship to "as above, so below." If all of capital "C" Creation is "God" and thus composed of "God" atoms and energy, then any fractal part of that "God" energy is therefore a part of God. Man is a fractal. Man is God. That is why Mack is told he is "a living fractal." That is why Mack is told that God is "in" all things.[14] The word fractal is being used as a pseudo-scientific synonym for the belief that God is "in" everything—everything being a fractal or a fractured part of the whole, a fractured part of God. Taken a step further, *The Shack* is indirectly presenting the notion that "chaos" is simply the result of people not seeing the "God in everything" fractal order in the world—"as above, so below."

Thus, *The Shack*—like Leonard Sweet's quantum spirituality—subtly introduces the New Age/New Spirituality as a worldview that puts forth the notion that "chaos" can be significantly overcome when humanity stops seeing itself as "separate"[15] but rather sees itself as "One"—as a part of the "God" who is "in" everyone and everything. However, the Bible teaches that humanity is not "God" or "One" with God (John 2:24-25; Ezekiel 28:2; Hosea 11:9, etc.). The Bible teaches just the opposite—that man is actually separated from God by sin (Isaiah 59:2). It is because of this "separation" that we need to acknowledge our sin and repent (Acts 2:38). Everyone must be born again (John 3:6-7)—born again from the God who is "above" (John 3:31), and not "below." Born again from the one true God—not by the "as above, so below" god that the Apostle Paul described as "the god of this world (2 Corinthians 4:4). The Bible states that we are only "one" in Christ Jesus (Galatians 3:28). And we are only "one" in Christ Jesus when we repent of our sins and accept His death on the cross for our sins (1 John 2:2)—his finished work on the cross of Calvary (Colossians 1:20).

"Chaos" is not created or furthered by humanity's denial of its so-called fractal divinity. The truth of the matter is that man is not divine—man is not God. Rather, "chaos" is the consequence of Adam's fall resulting in sinfulness and the subsequent decay of all things and our separation from a holy God. It is not "as above, so below." Fractals do not point the way to salvation. Genesis 11:6-8 warns about a deceptive and spiritually dangerous imagined "oneness":

> And the LORD said, Behold, the people is one, and they have all one language; and this they begin to do: and now nothing will be restrained from them, which they have imagined to do.

Acts 17:26 informs us that humanity is "one blood" and that we are connected to one another in that way. But humanity is not one Spirit. "That which is born of the flesh is flesh; and that which is born of the Spirit is spirit" (John 3:6). The Bible states that "flesh and blood cannot inherit the kingdom of God" (1 Corinthians 15:50). Jesus said, we "must be born again" (John 3:7).

God's creation is indeed intricate and wondrous. And in many countless ways it is beautifully and harmoniously interconnected—but it is not divine (Romans 1:25). Man is "fearfully and wonderfully made" (Psalm 139:14), but he is not a part of some divine fractal order. We are sinners and we need to be saved from the sin that separates us from God. It is as simple as that. Repenting and accepting Jesus Christ as our Lord and as the one and only Savior who saves us from our sins is the "narrow" and only way to eternal salvation (John 14:6; Matthew 7:13-14). The introduction of fractals in the story line of *The Shack* is a deceptive device to unsuspecting readers. It was an entry point into the pseudo-scientific notion of "fractal Oneness"—"as above, so below"/God "in" everything.

Bruce Lipton and As Above, So Below

Another reference to fractals and "as above, so below" was in a book titled *The Biology of Belief: Unleashing the Power of Consciousness, Matter & Miracles*. It was written by a Ph.D research scientist named Bruce H. Lipton. Lipton's book contains several passages where the author connects "as above, so below" not only to fractals, but also to quantum physics. This immediately clarifies what Leonard Sweet is doing in his book *Quantum Spirituality*. He is introducing the church to New Age quantum physics. It also probably clarifies why Eugene Peterson was led to insert "as above, so below" into the Lord's Prayer and why *The Shack* carries Peterson's endorsement on its front cover. *The Shack* is obviously a transformational device to slowly convert the reader to a new worldview based on a misapplication of quantum physics–the New Age/New Spirituality.

In an interview with Bruce Lipton, Lipton states that fractals are part of the "new math" that is the science behind the God "in" everything saying "as above, so below." He says:

> Inherent in the geometry of fractals is the creation of ever-repeating, "self-similar" patterns nesting within one another. You can get a rough idea of "repeating shapes" by picturing the popular toy, hand-painted Russian nesting dolls. Each smaller doll (structure) is a miniature, but not necessarily an exact version of the larger doll (form). This new math is the science behind the old saying, "As above, so below."[16]

I could see that Lipton's discussion of fractals, quantum physics, and cellular biology neatly dovetails with David Spangler's teachings on the cell and the New Age. Lipton's remarks also mesh with Leonard Sweet's "new cell theory" that is so integral to his quantum spirituality. Lipton states:

> In a fractal Nature, the appearances of structures

at any level of organization are "self-similar" to the structures found in higher or lower levels of organization. Therefore a fractal understanding of the organization at one level is applicable to understanding an organization at another level. When applied to the new biology, this new math reveals that a cell, a human and human civilization are "self-similar" images at different levels of organization. So by studying a cell, one can learn about a human. In studying the community of cells in a human body, one can learn the nature of forming a successful community of humans that form the larger organism, humanity. Perhaps we will find the answers to saving civilization through a study of the very successful cellular civilizations beneath our skin.[17]

After reading this, I reread the following from David Spangler's *The Reimagination of the World*:

To me, a more appropriate symbol for the New Age is the cell. The cell is really a living crystal. It possesses a highly structured internal order, yet this geometry is organized around information rather than around position, as in a crystal lattice. Protoplasm is highly dynamic; it can give birth to endless varieties of new life, yet it can also collect and focus energy in powerful ways. If we want to possess a magical crystal for our New Age work, we need look no further than our own bodies and the cells that make them up.[18]

I then reread how Leonard Sweet thanked David Spangler for helping him formulate his "new cell" understanding of New Light Leadership:

I am grateful to David Spangler for his help in formulating this "new cell" understanding of New Light leadership.[19]

I could see where all of this cellular discussion was going. Teilhard de Chardin, Matthew Fox, Leonard Sweet, and others with New Age affections are teaching the world and the church that God is "in" every atom—therefore God is "in" everything—therefore we are all One—"As above, so below." But in the Bible, the apostle Paul made it very clear to the Greek unbelievers on Mars Hill that while humanity shares one blood (Acts 17:26)—and all the cellular similarity that infers—humanity is still in need of a Savior. Sharing one blood implies a physical "oneness"—if you will—through our original parents, Adam and Eve. But Paul made it very clear that there is no spiritual oneness. After telling the Greeks that they shared one blood, he then told them about Jesus Christ. In Acts 17:31, in referring to God and Jesus Christ, he says:

> Because he hath appointed a day, in the which he will judge the world in righteousness by that man whom he hath ordained; whereof he hath given assurance unto all men, in that he hath raised him from the dead.

In Galatians 3:28, Paul clarifies that while we all share one blood with similar cellular composition, we are only one in Jesus Christ:

> There is neither Jew nor Greek, there is neither bond nor free, there is neither male nor female: for ye are all one in Christ Jesus.

Being one in Jesus Christ is not an automatic, universal oneness as Leonard Sweet in *Quantum Spirituality* and William Young in *The Shack* seem to suggest. Paul makes it very clear in Romans that Jesus Christ died for our sins, and when we accept and follow Him as our Savior, we are saved and set free from our sin:

> For all have sinned, and come short of the glory of God; Being justified freely by his grace through the redemption that is in Christ Jesus: Whom God has

set forth to be a propitiation through faith in his blood. (Romans 3:23-24)

For when we were yet without strength, in due time Christ died for the ungodly. (Romans 5:6)

But God commendeth his love toward us, in that, while we were yet sinners, Christ died for us. (Romans 5:8)

For the wages of sin is death; but the gift of God is eternal life through Jesus Christ our Lord. (Romans 6:23)

There is therefore now no condemnation to them which are in Christ Jesus, who walk not after the flesh, but after the spirit. (Romans 8:1)

Anticipating things like quantum physics and quantum spirituality, Paul warned Timothy not to become spiritually compromised by pseudo-scientific teachings—science falsely so-called.

O Timothy, keep that which is committed to thy trust, avoiding profane and vain babblings, and oppositions of science falsely so-called: Which some professing have erred concerning the faith. (1 Timothy 6:20)

Paul also warned Timothy there would come a time when men would follow false teachers who would turn them away from the one true God with their fractals and their fables—men like William Young and his book *The Shack*:

I charge thee therefore before God, and the Lord Jesus Christ, who shall judge the quick and the dead at his appearing and his kingdom; Preach the word; be instant in season, out of season; reprove, rebuke, exhort with all longsuffering and doctrine. For the time will come when they will not endure sound doctrine; but after their own lusts shall they heap to themselves teachers, having itching ears; And they shall turn away their ears from the truth, and shall be turned unto fables. (2 Timothy 4:1-4)

Exploring Off the Map

When Rick Warren endorsed colleague Bob Buford's book *Halftime* (a book dedicated to Peter Drucker), Warren said, "I want every man in my congregation to read this inspiring story!"[20] It was Buford, along with Norman Vincent Peale and others, who initially influenced Ken Blanchard with regard to the Lord. And it was Buford's Leadership Network that gave birth to the present-day emerging church movement and emerging leaders like Brian McLaren, Doug Pagitt, and Tony Jones. In May 2000, Leadership Network sponsored a conference titled "Exploring Off the Map." *Quantum Spirituality* author Leonard Sweet was a featured speaker at this conference with New Age sympathizers Ken Blanchard, Peter Senge, Margaret Wheatley, and others. Disregarding the certainty of God-given prophecy in Scripture, Leadership Network was determined to provide a more optimistic, user-friendly "map" to the future. For the conference, Sweet was given the lead role of Chief Scout.[21]

Margaret Wheatley, like Leonard Sweet, had been heavily influenced by quantum physics and the New Age. She was selected by New Age Marianne Williamson to write the last chapter for the book *Imagine: What America Could Be in the 21st Century: Visions of a Better Future from Leading American Thinkers.* This book is replete with articles by New Age authors and teachers like Deepak Chopra, Neale Donald Walsch, Barbara Marx Hubbard, and others. "Exploring off the Map" speaker Peter Senge also wrote a chapter for this New Age book that was being used as a fund-raiser for the Global Renaissance Alliance of New Age leaders.[22]

In the 2006 updated version of her 1992 book *Leadership and the New Science: Discovering Order in a Chaotic World,* Margaret Wheatley echoes the theme of the May 2000 Leadership Network Conference—"Exploring Off the Map." In her prologue titled "Maps to the Real World," we read:

> I have always thought of this book as a collection of intriguing maps, much like those used by the early explorers when they voyaged in search of new lands.[23]

It seems quite apparent that Wheatley's book *Leadership and the New Science* was the inspiration for the Leadership Network conference. She writes:

> In 1990, as I began to apply the new sciences to the challenges of leadership, I noted that "we live in a time of chaos, as rich in the potential for disaster as for new possibilities. . . ."
>
> Chaos and global interconnectedness are part of our daily lives . . . .
>
> It's time to realize that we will never cope with this new world using our old maps. It is our fundamental way of interpreting the world—our worldview—that must change.[24]
>
> Whatever your personal beliefs and experiences, I invite you to consider that we need a new worldview to navigate this chaotic time.[25]

Margaret Wheatley goes on to describe how "Quantum physics challenges our thinking about observation and perception, participation and relationships, and the influences and connections that work across large and complex systems."[26]

She then introduces readers to "Chaos Theory" and "fractals."
She states:

> Chaos is a necessary process for the creation of new
> order. . . . I also explore lessons to be learned from
> fractals—how nature creates its diverse and intricate
> patterns by the presence of a few basic principles.[27]

Wheatley explains that the first book she ever read on the
"new science" was written by Fritjof Capra—the New Age physicist who wrote *The Tao of Physics: An Exploration of the Parallels
between Modern Physics and Eastern Mysticism*. Wheatley writes:

> I opened my first book on the new science—Fritjof
> Capra's *The Turning Point*, which describes the new
> world view emerging from quantum physics. This
> provided my first glimpse of a new way of perceiving
> the world, one that comprehended its processes of
> change, its deeply patterned nature, and its dense
> webs of connections.[28]

Emerging church leader Brian McLaren, in his book *The
Church on the Other Side*, cites Margaret Wheatley and calls *Leadership and the New Science* an "inspiring book."[29] Commenting on
an anecdote from her book, McLaren mentions the emergence
of "quantum theory" to help people "cope with subatomic reality."[30] Several paragraphs after McLaren's reference to "quantum
theory," he identifies Rick Warren as one of the "gifted leaders
and wise writers" who is "helping us" to see where we need to go
in the future.[31] Shortly after that, in his book, McLaren refers to
the "Quantum leaps" that are moving us rapidly from one change
to another. He explains:

> We live in a time unlike any other time that any
> living person has known. It's not merely that
> things are changing. Change itself has changed,

> thereby changing the rules by which we live. . . .
> [T]here is more to this change than simply a linear
> extrapolation of rapid change and complexity.
> Quantum leaps are happening that are nothing like
> evolution. They remove us almost totally from our
> previous context.[32]

It is not at all surprising that those with New Age affections, like Leonard Sweet, Margaret Wheatley, Ken Blanchard, and Peter Senge, are integral parts of a conference titled "Exploring Off the Map." And it is not that surprising that emerging church leader Brian McLaren introduces Wheatley's book *Leadership and the New Science* and quantum physics into his writings. It seems clear that Leadership Network, with its ensemble of New Age sympathizers, is mapping out a more "positive" future for the church—one in which New Age quantum physics will be the definitive map—not the *Holy Bible*. Is it a coincidence that *The Shack's* main character, McKenzie Allen Phillips, has the initials M.A.P.? Maybe so. But certainly, *The Shack* when compared to the Bible is definitely "exploring off the map."

At the end of the posted online summary of the May 2000 "Exploring Off the Map" conference, several Leadership Network events were listed. Included on the list was a conference in Orlando, Florida that featured Rick Warren as the main speaker.[33] It would not be surprising if we were to find out that Warren had attended the "Exploring Off the Map" conference with Leonard Sweet and the others. Whatever the case, Rick Warren is no stranger to Bob Buford and the Leadership Network.[34]

The Quantum Revolution

Later, in following up on Bruce Lipton, I read his book *The Biology of Belief*. In my reading, I noticed that Lipton uses the term "quantum revolution" to describe the mounting enthusiasm building around quantum physics, the new biology, and the new worldview.[35] This seems to dovetail with the "new revolution"[36] author William

Young's narrator "Willie" advocated at the very end of *The Shack*. The author's enthusiastic call for a "new revolution" seems to be predicated on his earlier references to fractals,[37] science,[38] and "the quantum stuff that is going on at a subatomic level."[39] In other words, the new worldview—"God is "in" everything—"as above, so below." One thing is for sure—William Young's *The Shack* meshes perfectly with Leonard Sweet's quantum revolution and quantum spirituality. Is this "quantum revolution" the same "revolution" Rick Warren referred to when he turned to Ken Blanchard at the Birmingham Lead Like Jesus conference and said, "You know, Ken, let's start a revolution."?[40] Is this the "revolution" Warren claims will "change the world" and "change history"?[41] Is this "quantum revolution" the same "revolution" Brian McLaren, Erwin McManus, Shane Claiborne, and other emerging church leaders also refer to in their writings?[42] Time will tell.

It seems clear to me that quantum physics, the "new" biology, and the "new" math of fractal geometry are being used to provide a seemingly scientific basis for "proving" the "as above, so below" contention that God is "in" everything. We are being asked to believe that all of creation is an interconnected quantum field of energy and "oneness" that is "God." We are told that humanity will only survive and have a "positive future" if we recognize and play our part—as "God"—in this interconnected quantum "Field of Dreams." Rick Warren says "if you want Jesus to come back sooner, focus on fulfilling your mission."[43] In other words—"If you build it, he will come."[44] New Age matriarch Alice Bailey said, "His coming depends upon our work."[45] This sounds like Warren's P.E.A.C.E. Plan. And this sounds like Neale Donald Walsch's New Age PEACE Plan. As discussed at length in *Reinventing Jesus Christ* and *Deceived on Purpose*,[46] this is also the Peace Plan of the false Christ Maitreya—the New Age "Christ" who claims to already be here on earth waiting to be called forth—"If you build it, he will come." But the two big questions are: what God are we really talking about, and if we build it who is actually coming? Jesus Christ or Antichrist?

These PEACE Plans have something in common that unites them on a vital level—mysticism. Even Rick Warren promotes the same mystical spirituality that underlies the other plans. Warren sees Richard Foster's "spiritual formation" movement (i.e., contemplative spirituality) as a "valid message for the church" today.[47] But when one looks at Foster's spiritual formation, we see that the people he has drawn from support the very same view of God as Neale Donald Walsch and Alice Bailey. For instance, Foster often turns to the writings of Thomas Merton who says: "True solitude is a participation in the solitariness of God—Who is in all things."[48] Foster also draws from the late Catholic contemplative Basil Pennington, who expresses his God in everything views when he says that all religions "experience a deep unity" during meditation because "there is only one God to be experienced."[49] Foster's "spiritual formation" that Warren calls a "wake-up call" for "the body of Christ"[50] can be summed up in Tilden Edwards, whom Foster highly recommends, when Edwards states: "This mystical stream is the Western bridge to Far Eastern spirituality."[51]

"God's Dream" and Metaphysics

It seems that Leonard Sweet has a special role—much like Robert Schuller—to create a bridge from the church to the New Age/New Spirituality. It is not surprising that Sweet has been helped along and promoted by Schuller. Sweet is also promoted by a number of other church leaders including Rick Warren. In his 1999 book *SoulTsunami*, Sweet talks all about "God's Dream."[52] He also states that "physics is becoming metaphysics."[53] But it is not "God's Dream" that we accept this new worldview suggested by quantum physics and Sweet's New Age/quantum spirituality. God is not "in" everything and God does not dream. But rather God exposes false teachings and deceptive devices like the term "God's Dream."

Leonard Sweet's notion that "physics is becoming metaphysics" is similarly presented in an article titled, "As Above; So Below: The Mysteries of Quantum Metaphysics" by Richard and Iona

Miller.[54] Sweet's metaphysical/New Age statement is further underscored and exposed in an article written by Donald J. DeGracia Ph.D. who states that chaos, fractals, and quantum theory are intimately linked with the occult. In "Beyond The Physical: A Synthesis of Science and Occultism in Light of Fractals, Chaos, and Quantum Theory," DeGracia writes:

> Chaos, Fractals and Quantum Theory . . . These three branches of science contain principles identical to those found in occultism.[55]

> Landscheidt uses the ancient occult notion "as above, so below" (the Hermetic Axiom) to show how solar activities correlate with terrestrial activities. This research is a clear illustration of what I call the principle of the "Self-similarity of Nature," which means that the same principle of organization operates at different scales of Nature. This work also illustrates the compatibility of fractal and occult notions.[56]

After reading additional material related to fractals and quantum physics, I called Jennifer and thanked her for writing her article. I told her it had been very revealing and helpful. In another conversation with her, she added an interesting footnote to this whole subject of quantum physics and fractals. She informed me that Leonard Sweet had co-authored a book with emerging church leader Brian McLaren and Jerry Haselmayer titled *A is For Abductive: The Language of the Emerging Church*. The book is an alphabetized listing of various terms that have special significance to the emerging church. Under the letter "F" there is an entry for fractals, defining fractals as "The way in which the whole is replicated in miniature in every part."[57] In other words, "as above, so below"—God is "in" everything.

New Age "Oneness"

In the book *From the Ashes: A Spiritual Response to the Attack on America*, a cross-section of New Age and religious leaders (one of whom was Rick Warren) wrote various articles to encourage people after the tragic events of September 11, 2001. In an effort to create "order out of chaos," Neale Donald Walsch's article in that book challenges New Age and religious leaders everywhere to help save the world by preaching the New Age message that "we are all one." If everyone accepts this message, Walsch promises that "everything could change overnight." He explains:

> We must change ourselves. We must change the beliefs upon which our behaviors are based. We must create a different reality, build a new society . . . We must do so with new spiritual truths. We must preach a new gospel, its healing message summarized in two sentences:
>
> *We are all one.*
> *Ours is not a better way, ours is merely another way.*
>
> This 15-word message, delivered from every lectern and pulpit, from every rostrum and platform, could change everything overnight. I challenge every priest, every minister, every rabbi and religious cleric to preach this.[58]

But Walsch's New Age "God" has made it clear that "we are all one" because God is "in" everything. In prior books, Walsch quotes his "God" as saying:

> God *is* creation.[59]

> You are the Creator and the Created.[60]

> You are *already* a God. *You simply do not know it.*[61]

You are One with everyone and everything in the
Universe—including God.[62]

There is only One of Us. You and I are One.[63]

As previously mentioned, this is essentially the same God
"in" everything statement that can be found in *The Shack*,[64] *The
Purpose Driven Life*,[65] and the *The Message*.[66] Whether they realize
it or not, all three of these men—William Young, Rick Warren,
and Eugene Peterson—are giving Neale Donald Walsch and his
New Age "God" exactly what they want. Eugene Peterson has even
taken the "as above, so below" God "in" everything statement
he put in the Lord's Prayer to its logical New Age conclusion by
paraphrasing Ephesians 4:6 to read—"Everything you are and
think and do is permeated with Oneness."[67]

An interesting footnote: *The Shack's* author William Young
has actually stated online that the conversations of his characters in *The Shack* reflect actual "conversations" he has had with
"God."[68] He says his novel is only a novel in that he put what
"God" told him into a fictional story context. In other words,
statements such as "God, who is the ground of all being, dwells
in, around, and through all things" and references to "fractals"
and "the quantum stuff that is going on at a sub-atomic level" are
teachings that evolved from the "conversations" Young claims to
have had with "God." Young wrote that he had originally wanted
to title his book *Conversations with God* until he found out that
someone else (Neale Donald Walsch) had already written books
with that same title.[69]

Ironically, William Young actually has much in common
with Neale Donald Walsch. Not only do they both say they have
had real "conversations" with "God" and written about those
"conversations," but their "conversations" present many of the
same New Age/New Spirituality teachings. All of this begs the
question—just what "God" did William Young converse with?
It is safe to assume that the "God" that Young spoke with

is, in fact, the same "God" that Neale Donald Walsch spoke with in his "conversations." And this "God" is not the God of the Holy Bible but rather the "God" of the New Age/New Spirituality—the "God" the apostle Paul refers to with a small "g" as the "god of this world" (2 Corinthians 4:4) who is, of course, the one that our Lord and Savior, Jesus Christ, identifies as Satan.

Hidden in Plain Sight

I eventually rented the New Age movie that Jennifer refers to in her article and watched it for myself. In *The Seeker*, Will is a young boy who tries to save the world by finding the signs or "fractals" that have been hidden throughout time. At one point in the movie, Will and Merriman (one of the wise "Old Ones") have the following interchange:

> **Will:** Okay. Look at this. This pattern is a fractal. Its physics—My dad teaches this stuff. Like-like a hiding place that goes on and on forever.
>
> **Merriman:** Like a clue hidden in plain sight that declares the presence of a sign.[70]

Reflecting on what Merriman said, I had to ask myself—was Eugene Peterson's insertion of "as above, so below" into the Lord's Prayer in *The Message* like a New Age "fractal"—"a clue hidden in plain sight"? Was "as above, so below" in *The Message* a "clue" that would one day be regarded as a prophetic sign, like one of the hidden signs in the movie *The Seeker*? Would "as above, so below" be regarded in a New Age future as a fractal "message" from God—"the message" that was in *The Message*? Would this "as above, so below," God "in" everything fractal "message" of "oneness" be seen as the key to saving the world—just like the fractals in *The Seeker* and just as New Age leaders like Neale Donald Walsch are telling everybody? And would the "God in everything" quotes by Rick Warren in *The Purpose Driven Life*, by Leonard Sweet in *Quantum Spirituality*, and by William Young's "Jesus" in *The Shack* also be regarded one day as fractal clues that had been "hidden in plain sight" in their writings? Were these men all playing their unwitting part in the spiritual deception that Jesus warned would come in His name before His return when He stated, "Take heed that no man deceive you" (Matthew 24:4)?

One thing is for sure: God's true Holy Spirit would never inspire Eugene Peterson, Rick Warren, Leonard Sweet, William Young, or anyone else to put this "as above, so below," "God in everything," occultic (hidden) message teaching in any book that purposed to have anything to do with the one true God and His one true son, our Lord and Savior Jesus Christ.

A Stay-at-Home Mom

Jennifer, a stay-at-home mom, home schooling her fourteen year-old daughter, had done her homework. Her research had provided me with new insights regarding fractals, quantum physics, and their direct connection with the occult/New Age term "as above, so below." While Jennifer's insights about fractals and "as above, so below" had exposed an important New Age aspect of *The Shack,* it also helped to further expose Leonard Sweet's book *Quantum Spirituality* and the further New Age implications of Rick Warren's Purpose Driven movement.

Because of Jennifer's article, I had remembered Fritjof Capra's 1975 book *The Tao of Physics: An Exploration of the Parallels between Modern Physics and Eastern Mysticism.* It had been a cult classic when I was in the New Age movement many years ago. We had all been ready to take that big "quantum leap" into a peaceful New Age future when all the world would be as "One." Were books like Leonard Sweet's *Quantum Spirituality* and William Young's *The Shack* preparing the church to take that same quantum leap? All signs and fractals seemed to be pointing that way.

The New Age Implications of *The Shack*

New Age Belief	*The Shack*
God is the ground of all being—God is "in" all things.	"God," who is the ground of all being, dwells in, around, and through all things (p. 112).*
God indwells creation, therefore the word creation is frequently spelled with a capital "C."	The word creation is spelled with a capital "C" over twenty times.
Evil, darkness, Satan have no actual existence.	"Evil and darkness . . . do not have any actual existence" (p. 136). Satan is never mentioned.
Quantum Physics, chaos theory, fractal theory deceptively used by New Age and the Occult to try to scientifically "prove" that God is "in" everything because God is allegedly "in" every atom.	Subtly introduces quantum physics, chaos theory, fractal theory through references to "quantum stuff" (p. 95), "sub-atomic level" (p. 95), "chaos" (p. 128), and fractals (p. 129) while simultaneously teaching that God is "in" everything—including every atom (p. 112).
Bible is not inerrant and reliable. Mystical spiritual "experiences" with "God" are more authoritative—even if they conflict with Scripture.	The Bible is consistently devalued and marginalized. Mystical spiritual experiences with "God" more authoritative—even if they conflict with Scripture.

The Shack is described in the premier issue of Rick Warren's *Purpose Driven Connection* magazine as one of the "notable best-selling Christian books in 2008," and, as of this writing, it is being sold on the Purpose Driven Connection website: http://shop.purposedriven.com/The-Shack/A/0964729237.htm.

We have the epitome of a great science . . .

quantum physics . . .

Everyone is God.[1]

—New Age channeler J. Z. Knight
From *What the Bleep Do We Know!?*

Thirteen

The Quantum Leap to a New Age/New Spirituality?

The coming together of the new biology and the new physics is providing the basic metaphors for this new global civilization that esteems and encourages whole-brain experiences, full-life expectations, personalized expressions, and a globalized consciousness.[2]

—Leonard Sweet
SoulTsunami

When we experience such a quantum of transformation, we may simultaneously feel that the whole of the New Age is happening right now, that we are on the verge of overnight transformation—the fabled quantum leap into a new state of being.[3]

—David Spangler
Reimagination of the World

Saddleback Civil Forum and "Flip-Flopping"

On August 16, 2008, Rick Warren hosted the Saddleback Civil Forum with presidential candidates Barack Obama and John McCain. The Civil Forum was carried live on CNN and broadcast around the world. With Warren presiding, this venue was a distinct variation from the usual presidential debate format. During the event, Warren asked both men the same basic ten questions. One of these questions perhaps tells us more about Warren than either of the candidates answers did about them. Using slightly different wording, he asked both Barack Obama and John McCain to describe some position or belief they held ten years ago that they no longer hold today. He softened the question by stating that "sometimes flip-flopping is smart" because it's based on "additional information" and "knowledge." Warren said that changing one's position can often be viewed in a positive way. "That's not flip-flopping," he said. "Sometimes that's growing in wisdom." Here is how Warren approached the two presidential candidates on this matter of changing one's belief about something.

Rick Warren to Barack Obama:

A lot of times candidates are accused of flip-flopping, but actually sometimes flip-flopping is smart because you actually have decided on a better position based on knowledge that you didn't have.

What's the most significant position you held ten years ago that you no longer hold today, that you flipped on, you changed on, because you actually see it differently?[4]

Rick Warren to John McCain:

What is the most significant position that you've held, ten years ago, that you no longer hold today? I think the point I'm trying to make is that leaders are not stubborn. They do change their mind with additional information.

So give me a good example of something, ten years ago, you said that's the way I feel about and now, ten years later, I changed my position. That's not flip-flopping. Sometimes that's growing in wisdom.[5]

As I watched the Saddleback Civil Forum with my neighbors, I had to wonder if Rick Warren was introducing a rationale that he might end up using himself one day. For instance, this rationale could explain, in the future, why he was changing some of his views regarding biblical Christianity. For those who might accuse him of "heresy" or "flip-flopping," he would simply repeat what he told Barack Obama—"sometimes flip-flopping is smart because you actually have decided a better position based on knowledge that you didn't have." Or he could repeat what he told John McCain—"That's not flip-flopping. Sometimes that's growing in wisdom."

But what "additional information" could possibly cause Rick Warren to believe that some aspect of the Christian faith needed to be changed? What new "knowledge" could justify his adopting a new way of looking at biblical Christianity that, in effect, would result in his adopting a whole new worldview? Taken a step further, what new "knowledge" and "additional information" would help him to rationalize a new worldview that would mesh Christianity with the New Age/New Spirituality and other religions? The answer might very well come through the "new science" and the "new math"—quantum physics, chaos theory, and fractal theory—the "new science" attempt to scientifically prove that God is not only "transcendent" but also "immanent"—that God is "in" everything. Is this where Warren's Purpose Driven movement is actually heading?

The New Worldview?

Many prominent New Age figures have stated that the foundational teaching of the New World Religion is the "immanence" of God (i.e., God "in" everything). Benjamin Creme, New Age leader and spokesperson for the false New Age "Christ" Maitreya, says:

> But eventually a new world religion will be inaugurated which will be a fusion and synthesis of the approach of the East and the approach of the West. The Christ will bring together, not simply Christianity and Buddhism, but the concept of God transcendent— outside of His creation—and also the concept of God immanent in all creation—in man and all creation.[6]

New Age matriarch Alice Bailey also describes how the ultimate path to God in the New World Religion will be based on accepting the teaching of God's "immanence"—God "in" everything. Bailey writes:

> . . . a fresh orientation to divinity and to the acceptance of the fact of God Transcendent and of God Immanent within every form of life.
>
> These are the foundational truths upon which the world religion of the future will rest.[7]

Rick Warren's Saddleback Church *Foundations Participant's Guide* also uses these same terms—transcendence and immanence—to describe God. The guide's ambiguous wording regarding the word "immanent" could one day be interpreted to mean that God is "in" everything. This would be consistent with Warren's statement in *The Purpose Driven Life* where he states that the Bible says God is "in everything."[8] These statements in the *Participant's Guide* and in *The Purpose Driven Life* leave plenty of wiggle room for Warren down the line—should he continue to move in the direction of the New Spirituality/New World Religion. The Saddleback Church *Foundations Participant's Guide* states:

> The fact that God stands above and beyond his creation does not mean he stands outside his creation. He is both transcendent (above and beyond his creation) and immanent (within and throughout his creation).[9] (parentheses in original)

Robert Schuller has already publicly aligned himself with this foundational teaching of the New World Religion. On November 9, 2003, in an *Hour of Power* sermon broadcast to millions of people around the world, Schuller stated that over the previous several years his increased understanding of God's "immanence" had caused his faith to become "deeper, broader, and richer more than ever." He then proclaimed:

God is alive and He is in every single human being![10]

As already mentioned, Leonard Sweet presents this same teaching of immanence in his book *Quantum Spirituality*. While Sweet praises, promotes and even consults with New Age leaders, he also teaches that God is immanent—"in the very substance of creation [panentheism]."[11] And as previously mentioned, Eugene Peterson's "as above, so below" in the Lord's Prayer carries this same immanent God "in" everything message.[12]

If this immanent "God in everything" new worldview is where the church is heading, how might church leaders like Rick Warren present this view without looking like they've "flip-flopped" on their Christian faith? Again, the answer seems to be the intent to wed this God "in" everything immanence with the "new science" and the "new math." In other words, new findings from fractal theory, chaos theory, and quantum physics will seem to prove that God is "in" everything—"as above, so below." Given that Leonard Sweet's quantum spirituality may signify where Warren and other church leaders are headed, it is important to take a closer look at how New Age leaders are presenting *their* quantum spirituality.

The Quantum Christ

The New Age/New Spirituality is already heralding quantum physics as a "scientific" basis for their contention that God is not only transcendent but also immanent—"in" everyone and everything. Physicist Fritjof Capra's 1975 best-selling book on quantum physics—*The Tao of Physics: An Exploration of the Parallels between Modern Physics and Eastern Mysticism*—was the first to present this proposed scientific/spiritual model to a mass audience. In it, Capra explains that he gained new spiritual insights through a mystical experience he had sitting on a beach in Santa Cruz, California in 1969:

Five years ago, I had a beautiful experience which set me on a road that has led to the writing of this book. I was sitting by the ocean one late summer afternoon, watching the waves rolling in and feeling the rhythm of my breathing, when I suddenly became aware of my whole environment as being engaged in a gigantic cosmic dance. . . . As I sat on that beach my former experiences [research in high-energy physics] came to life; I 'saw' cascades of energy coming down from outer space, in which particles were created and destroyed in rhythmic pulses; I 'saw' the atoms of the elements and those of my body participating in this cosmic dance of energy; I felt its rhythm and I 'heard' its sound, and at that moment I *knew* that this was the Dance of Shiva, the Lord of Dancers worshipped by the Hindus.[13]

Commenting on his experience thirty years later, Capra writes that back in 1970 he "knew with absolute certainty that the parallels between modern physics and Eastern mysticism would someday be common knowledge.[14] In 1999, in a twenty-fifth anniversary edition of his book, Capra reflects on the fact that *The Tao of Physics* had sold more than a million copies over the years and had been translated into at least twelve languages:

What did *The Tao of Physics* touch off in all these people? What was it they had experienced themselves? I had come to believe that the recognition of the similarities between modern physics and Eastern mysticism is part of a much larger movement, of a fundamental change of worldviews, or paradigms, in science and society, which is now happening throughout Europe and North America and which amounts to a profound cultural transformation. This transformation, this profound change of consciousness, is what so many people have felt intuitively over the past two or three decades, and this is why *The Tao of Physics* has struck such a responsive chord.[15]

Capra adds:

> The awareness of the unity and mutual interrelation of all things and events, the experience of all phenomena as manifestations of a basic oneness, is also the most important common characteristic of Eastern worldviews. One could say it is the very essence of those views, as it is of all mystical traditions. All things are seen as interdependent, inseparable, and as transient patterns of the same ultimate reality.[16]

Fritjof Capra then describes the union of mysticism and the new physics as the "new spirituality" that is "now being developed by many groups and movements, both within and outside the churches." As an example of how this "new spirituality" is moving into the church, he refers to one of Leonard Sweet's "role models" and "heroes"—Matthew Fox:

> On the other hand, I also believe that our own spiritual traditions will have to undergo some radical changes in order to be in harmony with the values of the new paradigm. The spirituality corresponding to the new vision of reality I have been outlining here is likely to be an ecological, earth-oriented, postpatriarchal spirituality. This kind of new spirituality is now being developed by many groups and movements, both within and outside the churches. An example would be the creation-centered spirituality promoted by Matthew Fox and his colleagues.[17]

A perfect example of Capra's reference to how this quantum "new spirituality" is being developed in churches is exemplified by Margaret Wheatley's appearance at the Leadership Network's

May 2000 "Exploring off the Map" conference with Leonard Sweet and others. As described in the previous chapter, Wheatley first encountered the "new science" in Fritjof Capra's book *The Turning Point*, as noted in the updated introduction of her book *Leadership and the New Science*:

> I opened my first book on the new science—Fritjof Capra's *The Turning Point*, which describes the new world view emerging from quantum physics. This provided my first glimpse of a new way of perceiving the world, one that comprehended its processes of change, its deeply patterned nature, and its dense webs of connections.[18]

To further illustrate how pervasive this quantum spirituality has become in the church, consider an organization called VantagePoint3. This South Dakota-based group has developed a three-phase "spiritual formation" program called The VantagePoint3 Process (or L3), which incidentally is being used by a growing number of churches across North America. In the first phase—"Emerging Leaders"—a quote and summation of Margaret Wheatley is used to teach one of the points in that phase. The curriculum quotes Wheatley from her book *Leadership and the New Science* and emphasizes her view on "relationship" and "interconnection."[19] The fact that this program points to Wheatley demonstrates yet another way that quantum physics and quantum spirituality is already in the church. It is worth noting that this curriculum uses Galatians 3:27-28 to partially summarize what Wheatley has to say. But while Galatians 3 speaks of "Christ Jesus," Wheatley's quantum "Christ" is the universal "Christ" of quantum "oneness." VantagePoint3's use of Wheatley to teach about "Christ" is a perfect example of what Fritjof Capra described as this new spirituality being developed within the churches.

The VantagePoint3 Process also cites materials by Leonard Sweet, Peter Senge, and Ken Blanchard. All three were featured with Wheatley at the "Exploring off the Map" conference organized by Bob Buford and Leadership Network.

Another example of how quantum physics has already entered the church is through the ministry of Annette Capps—the daughter of best-selling author and charismatic pastor Charles Capps. There are over 100,000 copies of Annette Capps' booklet *Quantum Faith* in print. In the booklet, she presents a Christian faith compatible with the so-called "scientific" principles of quantum physics and as such is also compatible with the so-called "scientific" principles of the New Age/New Spirituality. She even refers readers to New Age leader Gary Zukav's book *The Dancing Wu Li Masters—An Overview of the New Physics.*[20] In her booklet, she writes:

> As I studied the theories of quantum physics, I was reminded of a prophecy given by my father, author and teacher Charles Capps, "Some things which have required faith to believe will no longer require faith, for it will be proven to be scientific fact."[21]

Obviously, authors like Gary Zukav and Fritjof Capra have had a huge influence not only in the world, but also in the church. Capra, a New Age physicist and Aquarian conspirator, is mentioned frequently in Marilyn Ferguson's book *The Aquarian Conspiracy.*[22] In addition, countless books and articles have been written about the quantum aspects of the "new science" and the "new spirituality" since the publication of Capra's *The Tao of Physics* and *The Turning Point.* Gary Zukav and his writings on quantum physics were praised and featured years ago by Oprah Winfrey on the *Oprah Winfrey Show.*[23] William Young's best-selling book *The Shack* is just the latest in a long line of books that deal directly or indirectly with quantum physics and quantum spirituality. And like Wheatley's book *Leadership and the New Science* but on a much larger scale, Young's book is also having great influence by subtly introducing quantum physics and quantum spirituality into the church. To top this off, a New Age movie on quantum physics has greatly influenced many people and has already become an underground cult classic.

What the Bleep Do We Know!?

The 2006 movie titled *What the Bleep Do We Know!?* was entirely devoted to the subject of quantum physics in an obvious effort to convert viewers to a New Age/New Spirituality/New Worldview. The movie was shown in major movie theaters around the country and can now be rented in video stores almost everywhere. In the movie, Ph.D. physicists and other "experts," teamed up with occult/channeler J. Z. Knight to use quantum physics to present their New Age/New Worldview that we are all "one" because God is "in" everything. The movie strongly conveys the idea that inner peace and world peace can be attained through a simple understanding of quantum physics. *What the Bleep Do We Know!?* contends that quantum physics proves that all creation is interconnected at the deepest sub-atomic level. Ph.D. physicist Amit Goswami—sounding more like Robert Schuller than a physicist—states that quantum physics is the "physics of possibilities."[24] With Schulleresque teachings about "Possibility Thinking" hanging in the air, Dr. Goswami contends that the principles of quantum physics can help each person create his or her own reality. He states:

> It may sound like a tremendous bombastic claim by some New Ager without any understanding of physics whatsoever, but really, quantum physics is telling us that.[25]

By making the speculative "quantum leap" from physics to metaphysics, *What the Bleep Do We Know!?* argues that as humanity comes to recognize that "we are all one" because God is "in" everything, then mankind—collectively as "God"—can and will create a positive, peaceful future. In the movie, New Age channeler J. Z. Knight channels an allegedly ancient spirit named "Ramtha." This familiar spirit proceeds to provide what seems to be spiritual corroboration for the "experts" in the movie. In an attempt to unite science and the New Age in an irrefutable quantum way, the channeled Ramtha makes these comments:

> We have the epitome of a great science . . . quantum
> physics . . . Everyone is God.[26]

Quantum Physics and the New Age "God"

Neale Donald Walsch and his New Age "God" also describe quantum physics as the scientific means for justifying the New Spirituality. Walsch's "God" positively references the Systems Theory popularized by business guru and Rick Warren "mentor" Peter Drucker to make his "quantum" point. Walsch's "God" describes God as a "System" with a capital "S."[27] The New Age "God" states that we are all "one" because we are all part of the universal energy of "God" the "System." "God" proceeds to tell Walsch and Walsch's countless readers that the purposeful, driving force of the "System" comes from all the quantum "parts" recognizing their quantum "oneness" with "God" the "System." But Walsch's "God" also warns about the danger of people seeing themselves as "separate" and not "part" of "God" the "System." Walsch and his "God" have the following interchange:

> **"God":** And, of course, the intelligence IS coming from you. It's coming from the *part* of you that is *me.* That is, it's coming from the System, of which you are an intrinsic part.
>
> But when an energy unit such as yourself sees itself as *not* part of the System at all, but as *a product* OF *the System,* the Life Form has created an illusion . . . .
>
> **Walsch:** And then along comes chaos theory and quantum physics.
>
> **"God":** Yes. And quantum physics is simply the scientific explanation for how God—"the System," if you please—looks at Its individual parts and watches Itself impacting those Parts.

You would call this phenomenon, in spiritual terms, a "higher level of consciousness," or "increased self-awareness." It is when That Which Is Aware experiences the fact that It affects that of which It IS aware.

Walsch: "Nothing which is observed is unaffected by the observer." The first law of quantum physics.[28]

The new worldview of the New Age/New Spirituality argues that for the good of the world and for a positive peaceful future, humanity must come to recognize that we are all "one" because we are all "part" of the quantum field or "System" that is "God." By seeing yourself as part of God—"the System"—you will ultimately save yourself and save the world. This is the New Paradigm. This is the New Age/New Spirituality described by quantum physics. This is the new emerging worldview. And this is the lie. It is the serpent in the Garden of Eden all over again.

Quantum Physics and John Marks Templeton

The late financier, philanthropist, and New Age sympathizer John Marks Templeton (and his foundation—the Templeton Foundation) have spent millions of dollars for several decades supporting individuals and organizations that attempt to use science to explain and prove theology—but a theology compatible with Templeton's New Age/New Spirituality affections. Neale Donald Walsch has described Templeton as his "wonderful role model."[29] He even patterned his 5-step New Age PEACE Plan after Templeton's "Humility Theology."[30] Templeton's book *The Humble Approach: Scientists Discover God* is a direct challenge pressuring Christians to disbelieve the absolute authority of Scripture. It subtly cajoles them to be "humble" enough to open themselves up to the new findings in science—new findings, as in quantum physics, that might provide them with a new approach to God and life—a new worldview. Walsch's New Age PEACE Plan, like Templeton's "Humble Approach," specifically asks people to admit that "some of our old beliefs about God and about life are no longer working."[31] He urges us to therefore "explore the possibility that there is something we do not understand about God and about life, the understanding of which could change everything."[32] His challenge is: are "we willing for new understandings of God and life to now be brought forth, understandings that could produce a new way of life on this planet."[33] In his book *The Humble Approach*, Templeton also urges his readers to be open to "strange new ideas."[34] He writes:

> God is five billion people on Earth and He is much more. . . . God is all of you and you are a little part of Him.[35]

> Differing concepts of God have developed in different cultures. No one should say that God can be reached by only one path.[36]

> Scriptures have been very beneficial to the whole world, but I am hoping we can develop a body of knowledge about God that doesn't rely on ancient revelations or scripture.[37]

Christian apologist Dave Hunt describes Templeton's heretical New Age beliefs and his connections to Robert Schuller:

> Templeton and his neopagan views were first introduced to the church in 1986 by Robert Schuller, who continues to endorse him. Schuller's *Possibilities* magazine put Templeton's picture on its front cover, and it's major article was an interview with Templeton. In it he expressed his Unity/Religious Science/New Age beliefs: "Your spiritual principles attract prosperity to you . . . material success . . . comes . . . from being in tune with the infinite. . . . The Christ spirit dwells in every human being whether the person knows it or not . . . nothing exists except

God." These heresies were promoted by Schuller to his vast audience of readers.[38]

In spite of Templeton's obvious New Age connections, Rick Warren seems to have no problem allowing himself to be a judge for the highly publicized "Power of Purpose Essay Contest" put on by Templeton and his well-funded organization. The million dollar "Templeton Prize for Progress in Religion" is given annually to people who have made a great contribution to the "progress" of religion. Over the last ten years, five of these awards were given to physicists, including the 2009 award which went to Bernard d'Espagnat, a French quantum physicist.

On the Templeton Press website, numerous books are available on "science and theology"—many of them related to quantum physics. One title, *Cosmic Dance: Science Discovers the Mysterious Harmony of the Universe*, is reminiscent of Fritjof Capra's description of quantum physics as a "cosmic dance of energy." Pastor Greg Boyd, who was once featured back to back with Rick Warren in an interview with Charlie Rose on PBS television,* has written a book (unpublished as of May 2009) about quantum physics tentatively titled *The Cosmic Dance*.

As stated earlier, John Marks Templeton's book *Discovering the Laws of Life* was endorsed and foreworded by the late Norman Vincent Peale. This book was Templeton's own personal take on the "Laws of Life." His laws and observations are frequently punctuated with quotes from influential New Age figures that include Unity minister Eric Butterworth, *A Course in Miracles* advocate Gerald Jampolsky, and spiritual medium Jane Roberts. In the foreword to Templeton's book, Peale wrote:

> I have known John Marks Templeton for many years and have admired him greatly. . . .
>
> Long before he reached his present success, John

---

*This interview took place on August 17, 2006.

> Templeton awakened spiritually . . . His most
> recent effort, the Humility Theology Information
> Center of the John Templeton Foundation, is
> typical, representing a commitment to discover
> and communicate the key factor in helping people
> develop humility, a spiritual quality that summarizes
> the character of Sir John.[39]

Norman Vincent Peale discloses in this foreword that, like Schuller, he had also interviewed John Marks Templeton for his church magazine:

> In an interview with the Peale Center's *Plus
> Magazine*, Sir John shared what he taught his own
> children about happiness.[40]

Birds of a Feather

While Norman Vincent Peale and Robert Schuller both had their own magazines, Rick Warren has now teamed up with Reader's Digest Association, Inc. to publish his own magazine titled *Purpose Driven Connection*. As I mentioned in the introduction, I learned that the late founder and longtime Executive Director of Reader's Digest, DeWitt Wallace, was a "good friend" of Norman Vincent Peale.[41] For nearly forty years, Reader's Digest published many of Peale's articles in their magazine.[42] In the book, *Theirs Was the Kingdom: Lila and DeWitt Wallace and the Story of Reader's Digest*, author John Heidenry writes:

> Norman Vincent Peale [was] a neighbor in nearby
> Pawling, no less, and a good friend of DeWitt
> Wallace. Peale preached a gospel—a way of life—called
> positive thinking. The message found in his best-
> selling *The Power of Positive Thinking*, published in
> 1952, was the same that the *Digest* itself had been
> preaching for thirty years.[43]

Reader's Digest was a perfect vehicle for Norman Vincent Peale, and it will be a perfect vehicle for Rick Warren too. In Templeton's book Discovering the Laws of Life, Templeton head-lined one of his important "laws of life" on page 69. In big bold black type it reads:

Birds of a feather flock together

Underneath this law, he included the following description:

Often we do search for groups that are like ourselves, and by joining these groups fulfill this law of life, by showing that indeed birds of a feather do flock together.[44]

Quantum Leap into the Future?

Leonard Sweet's book Quantum Spirituality was right up John Marks Templeton's quantum-physics alley. As far back as the 1991 publication of Quantum Spirituality, Sweet has been having a subtle, and sometimes not so subtle, "quantum" conversation with the church and its leaders. New Age author Gregg Braden describes this kind of conversation as a "quantum dialogue."[45]

In their 1995 joint presentation The Tides of Change, Leonard Sweet and Rick Warren had one of the subtler type quantum con-versations as they discussed "waves," "a new paradigm," and "this New Spirituality that we are seeing birthed around us."[46] When Warren stated that God works in "waves"—a significant term in quantum physics—Sweet jumped on the remark to describe the word "wave" as a "quantum metaphor." He then equated church growth with the "new science" of quantum physics:

> **Rick Warren:** Today we often have so little understanding of what God has done in the past. When you don't understand what God has done in the past, you don't realize that He does work in waves.

Leonard Sweet: That's right, yeah.

Rick Warren: That God has worked in many things that we often think are new, God is just doing again. And I believe that there can be waves of revival. There can be waves of renewal in the church. There can be waves of receptivity, when people are more open. . . .

And I think a lot of "church growth material" today is how to create a wave. And it can't be done. It is a sovereign move of God's Spirit. You know, you as a historian know about that. As we look at the '90s.

Leonard Sweet: Yeah, this is a wave period. I really love that metaphor of the wave and the wavelength. First of all, it is a quantum metaphor. It brings us out of the Newtonian world into this new science [quantum physics]. The other way I like about it so much, is that it brings us into the language of resonance. Wavelength.[47]

Rick Warren's collaboration with Leonard Sweet has endured through the years. As already stated, four years after *The Tides of Change* presentation, Warren endorsed Sweet's 1999 book *SoulTsunami*. In this book, Sweet invoked Robert Schuller's 1982 call for "God's Dream" and a "New Reformation" four years before Warren invoked the same terms to describe his Global P.E.A.C.E. Plan.[48] Clearly in sync with Schuller, and anticipating Warren to ride the same wave, Sweet said that "God's Dream" is to save the world by changing the future. In *SoulTsunami*, he writes:

> *SoulTsunami* is designed and dedicated not only to helping you predict, but to helping you intervene spiritually and socially to invent and prevent the future.[49]

Postmodern Christians are spiritual interventionists. The Postmodern Reformation Church will consciously intervene to help design this new world. There are many futures out there. The future is not a "single state," but a scenario of possibilities. There is a struggle between opposing visions of the future. It is not too late to choose which one we shall get. The future is a function of our choices and creations.[50]

He reiterated his hopes for the future of the church:

The future can no longer be an assumption. The future is now an achievement. There is a race to the future. Who will get there first? Will the Christian church? The time to save God's Dream is now. The people to save God's Dream are you.

This is an extraordinary moment in history. God wants you to do some extraordinary things. You can do some extraordinary things. Will you? The choice is yours.

God is birthing the greatest spiritual awakening in the history of the church. God is calling you to midwife that birth. Are you going to show up?[51]

Thus in 1999, Leonard Sweet stated that "God is birthing the greatest spiritual awakening in the history of the church." Is this the "New Spirituality" that Sweet mentioned to Rick Warren in their 1995 presentation that is being "birthed around us"? Is this "New Spirituality" the "God's Dream"/New Reformation/Revolution/Purpose Driven/ P.E.A.C.E. Plan for a "positive future" now being described by Warren and other church leaders? And if so, how will this positive future materialize? How will a "global civilization" with a "globalized consciousness" be created? In *SoulTsunami*, Sweet states that the "new biology" and the "new physics" hold the metaphysical key to the creation of this positive future—this global civilization. He explains:

> Physics is increasingly becoming the study of matter so small (is it a wave? is it a particle?) as to become the study of consciousness. In other words, physics is becoming metaphysics.[52]

> The coming together of the new biology and the new physics is providing the basic metaphors for this new global civilization that esteems and encourages whole-brain experiences, full-life expectations, personalized expressions, and a globalized consciousness.[53]

Quantum New Worldview

Leonard Sweet is definitely one of the point men for today's emerging/postmodern/Purpose Driven Church. As Rick Warren has aligned himself with Sweet, it is important to remember that Sweet has described former and present New Age figures as his "heroes" and "role models." He has openly acknowledged that his quantum "new cell theory" understanding of "new light leadership" was formulated with the help of veteran New Age leader David Spangler. Additionally, Sweet describes mystical New Age priest Pierre Teilhard de Chardin as "Twentieth-century Christianity's major voice."[54] And while Sweet's almost "in your face" New Age sympathies are there for all to see, Rick Warren, and other Christian figures continue to hold him in high esteem. But it is just business as usual as Warren's apologist tells us that "Doctrinally/theologically, Leonard Sweet is about as Christian as anyone can get."[55]

In his 2009 book *So Beautiful*, Leonard Sweet underscores his quantum "relational worldview"[56] by favorably quoting from William Young's *The Shack* regarding relationship.[57] He also tells readers to look to Margaret Wheatley's *Leadership and the New Science* to further understand his quantum view on the "spiritual and social significance of relationship."[58] And he still continues to refer readers back to his 1991 book, *Quantum Spirituality*.[59]

While appearing to be somewhat of a 21st century renaissance man who leaves everyone in the wake of his postmodern intellect, Leonard Sweet's "scientific" postmodern/quantum/New Age view on things raises some critical questions—particularly in regard to his association with Rick Warren. If Warren, Sweet, and other Christian leaders continue to move the church towards the New Spirituality, how will it ultimately play out? Will we see Warren, Schuller, Sweet, McLaren, and other "New Light" leaders signing a mutual accord someday affirming that God is "in" everything? Will that proclamation be based on new "scientific findings" from quantum physics? Will they explain that Pierre Teilhard de Chardin and the "God" of Neale Donald Walsch and William Young had it right—that "the sub-atomic reality" is that God is in every atom? That God really is—scientifically speaking—"in" everyone and everything?

But what about the inevitable reaction that will come from those referred to by Rick Warren as "fundamentalists"[60] when they accuse Warren of flip-flopping? Will Warren defend his new worldview by repeating what he said at the Saddleback Civil Forum—that "sometimes flip-flopping is smart because you actually have decided a better position based on knowledge that you didn't have"? Armed with seemingly scientific "facts" from quantum physics, will Warren defend his new worldview by stating, "That's not flip-flopping. Sometimes that's growing in wisdom"? Is this where Warren, Sweet, and other Christian leaders will try to take the church? Are they about to take a big "quantum leap" into the New Spirituality of a New Age that is based on the findings of the "new science"? Given the continued New Age implications of the emerging Purpose Driven movement, it would seem that this is a real possibility.

Fourteen

Rick Warren's "Broad Way" Christianity

Enter ye in at the strait gate: for wide is the gate,
and broad is the way, that leadeth to destruction,
and many there be which go in thereat.

—**Matthew 7:13**

Behold, they shall surely gather together, but not
by me.

—**Isaiah 54:15**

Rick Warren's Purpose Driven movement has, in a relatively short period of time, become what *TIME* magazine has referred to as a "Purpose Driven empire."[1] The word empire is defined in the dictionary as "supreme rule; absolute power or authority; dominion." It also means "an extensive social or economic organization under the control of a single person, family, or corporation."[2] For all intents and purposes, Rick Warren has become the titular head—the almost emperor-like CEO—of an increasingly apostate postmodern church. But while Warren continues to be embraced by much of the world and much of the church, it is not too late for people to reconsider their involvement with him and his Purpose Driven movement. Here are ten scripturally based reasons why people with any love of the truth should not involve themselves in Warren's "Broad Way" Christianity:

Ten Basic Reasons

1) Rick Warren's Purpose Driven movement offers a "Broad Way" Christianity. One of the mysteries of the Christian faith can be found in Jesus' warning that the way to life is "narrow" and that "few" would actually find it. Jesus is telling us in advance that the "broad way"—no matter how well intentioned—is not from Him. With Rick Warren's reformation movement based on deeds and not creeds, everyone is invited to partake in this global effort. But biblical principles are watered-down and often cast aside.

> Enter ye in at the strait gate: for wide is the gate, and broad is the way, that leadeth to destruction, and many there be which go in thereat: Because strait is the gate, and narrow is the way, which leadeth unto life, and few there be that find it. (Matthew 7:13-14)

2) Rick Warren's "Broad Way" Christianity does not declare "all the counsel of God." Rick Warren teaches only what he wants to teach from the Bible. As a result, there are many important teachings that he skips over, de-emphasizes, and leaves out—particularly in regard to prophecy and spiritual deception.

> For I have not shunned to declare unto you all the counsel of God. Take heed therefore unto yourselves, and to all the flock, over the which the Holy Ghost hath made you overseers, to feed the church of God, which he hath purchased with his own blood. For I know this, that after my departing shall grievous wolves enter in among you, not sparing the flock. Also of your own selves shall men arise, speaking perverse things, to draw away disciples after them. Therefore watch, and remember, that by the space of three years I ceased not to warn every one night and day with tears. (Acts 20:27-31)

3) Rick Warren's "Broad Way" Christianity does not discern the spiritual signs of the times. Just as the leaders in Jesus' day discerned the weather but not the signs of the times, Warren discerns many of the social and economic problems, but not the spiritual signs of the times.

> O ye hypocrites, ye can discern the face of the sky; but can ye not discern the signs of the times? (Matthew 16:3)

4) Rick Warren's "Broad Way" Christianity is ignorant of Satan's devices. Whereas the apostle Paul stated that he and other believers were "not ignorant of Satan's devices," Warren's "Broad Way" Christianity states that Satan's schemes are "entirely predictable."[3] By being ignorant of Satan's devices, this "Broad Way" Christianity has fallen prey to Satan's devices—particularly in the area of the New Age/New Spirituality/New Worldview.

> Lest Satan should get an advantage of us: for we are not ignorant of his devices. (2 Corinthians 2:11)

5) Rick Warren's "Broad Way" Christianity does not expose *spiritual* evil. Warren's version of Christianity does not sound a true warning about the deceptive spirit world and spiritual deception. There is much more to evil than the problems that Rick Warren is seeking to remedy with his Purpose Driven P.E.A.C.E. Plan. We are told to expose false prophets and false teachers, not to study under them, spiritually join with them, and further their plans.

> For we wrestle not against flesh and blood, but against principalities, against powers, against the rulers of the darkness of this world, against spiritual wickedness in high places. (Ephesians 6:12)

> But evil men and seducers shall wax worse and worse, deceiving, and being deceived. (2 Timothy 3:13)

> And have no fellowship with the unfruitful works of darkness, but rather reprove them. (Ephesians 5:11)

> For if the trumpet give an uncertain sound, who shall prepare himself to the battle? (1 Corinthians 14:8)

6) Rick Warren's "Broad Way" Christianity does not "earnestly contend for the faith." By not declaring all the counsel of God, by not discerning the signs of the times, by being ignorant of Satan's devices, and by not exposing spiritual evil, Rick Warren's "Broad Way" Christianity is not fighting "the good fight of faith."

> Beloved, when I gave all diligence to write unto you of the common salvation, it was needful for me to write unto you, and exhort you that ye should earnestly contend for the faith which was once delivered unto the saints. (Jude 3)

> Fight the good fight of faith, lay hold on eternal life, whereunto thou art also called, and hast professed a good profession before many witnesses. (1 Timothy 6:12)

> Wherefore take unto you the whole armour of God, that ye may be able to withstand in the evil day, and having done all, to stand. (Ephesians 6:13)

7) Rick Warren and his "Broad Way" Christianity are loved by the world and it's leaders. Jesus loved the world, but the world did not love Him. Jesus warned his followers they would be hated, persecuted, and even killed by the world—just as the world hated, persecuted, and killed Him. In his compromised effort to reach out to the world, Warren and his "Broad Way" Christianity have become the world.

They are of the world: therefore speak they of the world, and the world heareth them. (1 John 4:5)

Woe unto you, when all men shall speak well of you! for so did their fathers to the false prophets. (Luke 6:26)

Yea, and all that will live godly in Christ Jesus shall suffer persecution. (2 Timothy 3:12)

And ye shall be hated of all men for my name's sake. (Matthew 10:22)

If they have called the master of the house Beelzebub, how much more shall they call them of his household? (Matthew 10:25)

For what is a man advantaged, if he gain the whole world, and lose himself, or be cast away? (Luke 9:25)

8) Rick Warren's "Broad Way" Christianity is engaged in a process of ungodly change. Rick Warren describes himself as a "change agent" but in his attempt to change the world, he and his Purpose Driven movement are actually changing biblical Christianity. The Bible warns about those who push for unbiblical and ungodly change.

My son, fear thou the LORD and the king: and meddle not with them that are given to change. (Proverbs 24:21)

Jesus Christ the same yesterday, and to day, and for ever. (Hebrews 13:8)

For I am the LORD, I change not. (Malachi 3:6)

Behold, the days come, saith the Lord GOD, that I will send a famine in the land, not a famine of bread, nor a thirst for water, but of hearing the words of the LORD. (Amos 8:11)

9) Rick Warren's "Broad Way" Christianity is frequently "double-tongued" and "double-minded." Rick Warren's attempts to seemingly distance himself from the New Age/New Spirituality while simultaneously spiritually aligning himself with New Age sympathizers is "double-tongued," "double-minded," and deceptively self-serving. In the Psalms, David refers to those who speak with "flattering lips" and a "double heart."

> Help, LORD; for the godly man ceaseth; for the faithful fail from among the children of men. They speak vanity every one with his neighbor: with flattering lips and with a double heart do they speak. (Psalm 12:1-2)
>
> Likewise must the deacons be grave, not doubletongued, not given to much wine, not greedy of filthy lucre; Holding the mystery of the faith in a pure conscience. (1 Timothy 3:8-9)
>
> A double minded man is unstable in all his ways. (James 1:8)

10) Rick Warren's "Broad Way" Christianity is "not valiant for the truth." Warren has demonstrated, in numerous ways, that he is politically and spiritually expedient when it comes to the truth. His "Broad Way" Christianity plays to the world and embraces the world because it *is* the world. It does not hold fast to the truth because it is not "valiant for the truth."

> And they bend their tongues like their bow for lies: but they are not valiant for the truth upon the earth. (Jeremiah 9:3)
>
> If ye continue in my word, then are ye my disciples indeed; And ye shall know the truth, and the truth shall make you free. (John 8:31)

The Time is Here

The apostle Paul preached the importance of adhering to God's Word. He warned that the time would come when believers would not endure sound doctrine but would find teachers who would tell them what they wanted to hear:

> Preach the word; be instant in season, out of season; reprove, rebuke, exhort with all longsuffering and doctrine. For the time will come when they will not endure sound doctrine; but after their own lusts shall they heap to themselves teachers, having itching ears; And they shall turn away their ears from the truth, and shall be turned unto fables. (2 Timothy 4:3-4)

As Rick Warren's "broad way" Christianity seems to be headed down the "broad way" of the New Spirituality, it is very clear that his Purpose Driven movement is anything but the "narrow way" that Jesus Christ described in Matthew 7:14.

It is important to understand what is at stake here—the centrality of the Cross as the one and only true Gospel—without which the hope of salvation is lost. Jesus Christ, dying on the Cross for our sins, is the central message of the Gospel. It is the plumb line for ultimately discerning truth from error. But in discerning truth from error, it is essential that we must adhere to *all* the counsel of God (Acts 20:27).

Jesus is the one and only Savior—the one and only true Christ. Science cannot and will not prove otherwise (1 Timothy 6:20). God is not "in" everything. We are not Christ, and we are not God. What is born of the flesh is flesh. What is born of the Spirit is spirit. Flesh and blood cannot inherit the kingdom of God (1 Corinthians 15:50). It is not "as above, so below." The apostle John states:

> He that cometh from above is above all: he that is

of the earth is earthly, and speaketh of the earth: he
that cometh from heaven is above all. (John 3:31)

Jesus Christ is Lord. His name is above all names (Philippians
2:9). He is not the "Jesus" of *The Shack,* and He is not the "Jesus"
of the New Age/New Spirituality. Most assuredly, He is not the
"quantum Christ" of a deceived world and an apostate church.

The apostle Paul describes the simplicity of Christ (2 Corinthians 11:3). According to many of today's spiritual and religious
leaders, it has taken humanity 2000 years to finally "get it." They say
we need quantum physicists, cellular biologists, Ph.D. mathemati-
cians, New Age channelers, and emerging postmodern preachers
to finally understand what Jesus was trying to tell us back in the
first century. No, this is not the simplicity that Paul was describing.
This is the deceptive work of our Adversary as he tries to transform
the creation into the Creator and co-opt God's creation to himself.

Unfortunately, many of today's pastors have forgotten that
Satan is the god of this world (2 Corinthians 4:4) and that we
are to "stand against the wiles of the devil" (Ephesians 6:11). As a
result, the church is now catapulting into great spiritual deception.

For those who still rightly divide and depend upon the Word
of God, the Bible warns that the coming deception will be so great
that most of the world will be deceived (Revelation 13:13-14).
Jesus warned that His way is *not* the broad way but the "narrow
way" of continuing in His Word (John 8:31). And it is His way
that leads to eternal life.

> And when these things begin to come to pass, then
> look up, and lift up your heads; for your redemption
> draweth nigh. (Luke 21:28)

Epilogue

And his power shall be mighty, but not by his own power: and he shall destroy wonderfully, and shall prosper, and practise, and shall destroy the mighty and the holy people.

—Daniel 8:24

Sadly, Christian leaders today are in absolute denial about the New Age/New Spirituality that is accelerating its reach into the world and into the church. These leaders are telling us we need not be concerned about spiritual deception—or Antichrist, and they have all but forgotten the devices of the adversary. They say all the world needs to do is follow their lead, engage in their P.E.A.C.E. Plans, and be a part of a New Reformation that will change the world.

In an online update of *Reinventing Jesus Christ*, I relayed a conversation my wife and I had not long after our conversion: We talked about the ultimate spiritual deception described in the Bible—the great "falling away" of the church and the coming of Antichrist. We agreed that for someone like Antichrist to be credible in the world, he would need a majority of the people who call themselves Christians to believe that he is Christ. If he could get enough Christians—especially influential Christian leaders—to follow him, he could then discredit and marginalize those who oppose him. But to get people who call themselves Christians to believe he is Christ, he would first have to successfully redefine Christianity. To do that he would have to introduce non-Christian teachings and practices into the church, while at the same time make them appear Christian. His obvious goal would be to convert undiscerning and unsuspecting believers into a more eastern and mystical, New Age "Christianity." While invoking the name of "God" and "Christ," he would actually turn the Bible upside down—just as we had seen in our New Age teachings.

For this end-time, world-wide deception to take place, Christianity would have to become a more "positive" New Age "Christianity." This emerging New Age Christianity would have "a form of godliness" but it would actually deny the true faith (2 Timothy 3:5). This New Age Christianity/New Spirituality would use Christian terminology, while being under the spell of "another Jesus," "another spirit," and "another gospel" (2 Corinthians 11:4). This New Age/New Gospel/New Spirituality would be the ultimate counterfeit and the ultimate deception. It would be what the real Jesus warned His followers to watch out for.

In Conclusion

So where is this ever-expanding Purpose Driven movement heading, and how will it get there? I believe with all of my heart that Rick Warren and his colleagues are being used to lead the church into a New Spirituality for a New Age. Whether they consciously realize this or not is beside the point. The fact is they are doing it, and it has become a mockery of those who came before them and who rightly divided the Word of God—men and women who willingly died for their faith rather than compromise themselves with the world.

For over four years, I have watched as Rick Warren and his Saddleback apologists have attempted to refute any and all of the legitimate concerns that have been raised by so many of us. They have not only sought to discredit those who presumed to question Warren but have sought to discredit even a man like George Mair, whose genuine praise of Warren did not happen to suit their purposes.

Rick Warren is most definitely a man with a purpose. However, Proverbs 15:22 warns—"without counsel purposes are disappointed." As self-appointed peace ambassadors approach the church from all sides, let us not make the mistake Joshua made. He took the deceptive peace ambassadors from the land of Gibeon at their word "and asked not counsel at the mouth of the Lord" (Joshua 9:14). Putting unwarranted trust in their word, Joshua made peace with these deceivers and learned a hard lesson: We must always seek the "counsel" of the Lord.

It is imperative that believers who are "valiant for the truth" (Jeremiah 9:3) seek the Lord's counsel regarding the New Spirituality that is coming through the emerging Purpose Driven movement, Rick Warren, and other Christian leaders. Proverbs 14:12 warns that "There is a way which seemeth right unto a man, but the end thereof are the ways of death." Remember James 1:5: "If any of you lack wisdom, let him ask of God, that giveth to all men liberally, and upbraideth not; and it shall be given him."

The Bible warns in Matthew 13:20-21, Mark 4:16-17, and Luke 8:13 that many who receive the Lord with "gladness" and "joy" fall away in times of persecution, affliction, tribulation, and temptation. It is not enough to say "Lord, Lord"—we must follow the true Jesus Christ. And by His grace and sufficiency, we must seek to do His will and not the will of our spiritual adversary or the will of compromised leaders. Jeremiah warned of a "wonderful and horrible" deception (Jeremiah 5:30). In a time such as this, let us heed our Lord's words in Luke 21:8 that we "take heed" and "be not deceived."

May God bless and keep you during these perilous and turbulent times. May the love of God and the love of the truth always be first and foremost in your heart and in your prayers. He has promised that by His grace, we *shall* stand.

> Therefore being justified by faith, we have peace with
> God through our Lord Jesus Christ: By whom also we
> have access by faith into this grace wherein we stand,
> and rejoice in hope of the glory of God. (Romans 5:1-2)

ENDNOTES

Preface

1. Statistics taken from Rick Warren's website at: http://www.rickwarren.com/about.html.

2. Timothy C. Morgan, "Purpose Driven in Rwanda" (*Christianity Today*, October 2005, http://www.christianitytoday.com/ct/2005/october/17.32.html).

Introduction

1. November 24, 2008, press release: A. Larry Ross and Whitney Kelly, "Rick Warren and Reader's Digest Association Create a Multi-Platform Partnership To Serve Purpose Driven Readers: New Purpose Driven Connection to Deliver Spiritual Content and Community in Category-Busting Formats Worldwide," http://www.rickwarrennews.com/081124_readers_digest.htm.

2. John Heidenry, *Theirs Was The Kingdom: Lila and DeWitt Wallace & The Story of the Reader's Digest* (New York, NY: W.W. Norton & Company, 1993), p. 252; book was brought to my attention by Discernment Ministries.

3. Information provided by Reader's Digest Association Inc. via a telephone conversation with Warren Smith, April 2009.

4. John Heidenry, *Theirs Was The Kingdom*, op. cit, p. 282; Bob Thompson, "Richard Nixon and the Oobie-Doobie Girl" (*Washington Post Magazine*, July 27, 1997, http://comcast.rayconiff.info/media.html).

5. A. Larry Ross, "Rick Warren and Reader's Digest Association Create A Multi-Platform Partnership to Serve Purpose Driven Readers," op. cit.

6. Dan Wooding, "Rick Warren Hits Home Run With Announcement of Global Peace Plan to Battle Giants of Our World" (*Assist News*, April 17, 2005, http://www.cephas-library.com/purposedriven/purposedriven_warren_hooks_the_church_up_with_the_un.html), Wooding quoting Warren at the 25th anniversary celebration at Angel Stadium. Warren also uses the term "change agent" on page 20 of his book *The Purpose Driven Church*.

1/Deceived on Purpose

1. Rick Warren, *The Purpose Driven Life: What on Earth Am I Here For?* (Grand Rapids, MI: Zondervan, 2002), pp. 30-31; Bernie Siegel, *Love, Medicine & Miracles* (New York, NY: Harper-Collins Publishers: HarperPerennial, 1998), pp. 18-20; Warren Smith, *Deceived on Purpose:*

The New Age Implications of the Purpose Driven Church (Magalia, CA: Mountain Stream Press, 2004), pp. 47-49.

2. Warren Smith, *Deceived on Purpose*, op. cit., pp. 155-159.

3. Rick Warren, *The Purpose Driven Life*, op. cit., p. 88.

4. Warren Smith, *Deceived on Purpose*, op. cit., p. 82.

5. Rick Warren, *The Purpose Driven Life*, op. cit., p. 19 (footnote #3), p. 20 (footnote #6), p. 31 (footnote #11).

6. Ronald S. Miller and the Editors of *New Age Journal, As Above, So Below: Paths to Spiritual Renewal in Daily Life* (Los Angeles, CA: Jeremy P. Tarcher, Inc., 1992), p. xi, quoted in Warren Smith, *Deceived on Purpose*, op. cit., p. 32.

7. Ibid.

8. "As Above, So Below" (http://www.themystica.com/mystica/articles/a/below_above.html).

9. See: http://www.mothermaryspeaks.com/as_above_so_below.htm.

10. Eugene H. Peterson, *The Message* (Colorado Springs, CO: Nav-Press), Ephesians 4:6.

11. Rick Warren, *The Purpose Driven Life*, op. cit., p. 285.

12. Warren Smith, *Deceived on Purpose*, op. cit., p. 146.

13. Ibid., p. 147.

14. Ibid., p. 148.

15. "2004 Robert H. Schuller Institute" (*Powerlines: Monthly News for Hour of Power Spiritual Shareholders and Friends*, http://web.archive.org/web/20031017043658/www.hourofpower.org/powerlines/09.03/2004_robert_schuller_institute.cfm); Warren Smith, *Deceived on Purpose*, op. cit., p. 103.

16. Robert H. Schuller, "What Will Be the Future of This Ministry?" (*Hour of Power*, Program #1783, April 4, 2004, http://web.archive.org/web/20051125132928/www.hourofpower.org/booklets/bookletdetail.cfm?ArticleID=2570); Warren Smith, *Deceived on Purpose*, op. cit. p. 103.

17. Tim Stafford, "A Regular Purpose Driven Guy" (*Christianity Today*, November 18, 2002, Vol. 46, No. 12, http://www.christianitytoday.com/ct/2002/012/1.42.html); Warren Smith, *Deceived on Purpose*, op. cit., pp. 103-104.

18. Robert H. Schuller, *Self-Esteem: The New Reformation* (Waco, TX: Word Books, 1982), p. 19; Warren Smith, *Deceived on Purpose*, op. cit., p. 53.

19. Rick Warren, *The Purpose Driven Life*, op. cit., p. 31; Warren Smith, *Deceived on Purpose*, op. cit., p. 53.

20. Rick Warren, *The Purpose Driven Church: Growth Without Compromising Your Message & Mission* (Grand Rapids, MI: Zondervan, 1995), p. 398; Warren Smith, *Deceived on Purpose*, op. cit., pp. 105-106.

21. Robert H. Schuller, *Your Church Has A Fantastic Future!: A Possibility Thinker's Guide To A Successful Church* (Ventura, CA: Regal Books, 1986), p. 235; Warren Smith, *Deceived on Purpose*, op. cit., pp. 105-106.

22. Warren Smith, *Deceived on Purpose*, op. cit., p. 103.

23. Robert Schuller, *Self-Esteem: The New Reformation*, op. cit., p. 25.

24. Ibid., p. 104.

25. "Myths of the Modern Megachurch" (Pew Forum on Religion, Monday, May 23, 2005, Key West, Florida, http://pewforum.org/events/index.php?EventID=80).

26. Rick Warren, Saddleback Church e-mail, October 27, 2003, "GOD'S DREAM FOR YOU–AND THE WORLD!," all capital letters in original e-mail; Warren Smith, *Deceived on Purpose*, op. cit., Chapter 12, "Rick Warren's P.E.A.C.E. Plan."

27. Ibid.

28. Warren Smith, *Deceived on Purpose*, op. cit., p. 142.

29. "THE FIVE STEPS TO PEACE," Conversations with God website; (http://www.cwg.org/5steps/5stepstopeace.pdf).

30. Warren Smith, *Deceived on Purpose*, op. cit., p. 134.

31. Neale Donald Walsch, *The New Revelations: A Conversation with God* (New York, NY: Atria Books, 2002), p. 281; Warren Smith, *Deceived on Purpose*, op. cit., pp. 65-67.

32. Ibid., pp. 281-282.

33. Ibid., p. 282.

34. Ibid.

35. Ibid.

36. Ibid.

37. Bernie Siegel endorsed Robert Schuller's 1995 book *Prayer: My Soul's Adventure with God*; Gerald Jampolsky endorsed Robert Schuller's 2005 book *Don't Throw Away Tomorrow: Living God's Dream for Your Life*.

38. Lydia Rose Proenza, "Jerry Jampolsky, MD & Diane Cirincione" (*Hour of Power*, http://www.hourofpower.org/interviews/interviews_detail.cfm?ArticleID=3079).

39. Robert Schuller, *Self-Esteem: The New Reformation*, op. cit., pp. 51, 123.

40. Personal notes from Johanna Michaelsen's telephone call to the Crystal Cathedral on October 3, 1985. Used with permission; Warren Smith, *Deceived on Purpose*, op. cit., pp. 92-93.

41. Robert H.Schuller, *The Be (Happy) Attitudes: Eight Positive Attitudes that Can Transform Your Life!* (New York,NY: Bantam Books, 1985), p. 150; Warren Smith, *Deceived on Purpose*, op. cit., pp. 90-100.

42. Warren Smith, *Deceived on Purpose*, op. cit., p. 48.

43. Ibid., p. 113.

44. Ibid., p. 171.

45. Ibid.

46. Ibid., p. 71.

47. Ibid., p. 178.

48. Ibid., pp. 179-180.

49. Rick Warren, *The Purpose Driven Church*, op. cit., p. 69.

2/Saddleback Responds

1. Gilbert Thurston, former 40 Days of Purpose Field Representative, "Response to *Deceived on Purpose* by Warren Smith." On file. This was the initial Saddleback report that was e-mailed to people inquiring about *Deceived on Purpose*.

2. March 2, 2005 e-mail inquiry from an Evangelical pastor in Winston, Oregon to Saddleback pastoral staff, given to me by a member of the Winston church. On file.

3. March 3, 2005 e-mail reply to pastor in Winston, Oregon from Saddleback staff member Dan Hurst, given to me by a member of the Winston church. On file.

4. Gilbert Thurston, "Response to *Deceived on Purpose* by Warren Smith," op cit.

5. Ibid.

6. Ibid.

7. Richard Abanes, "Warren Smith, the New Age, and Deception," p. 1. This is a report by Rick Warren's apologist originally located on the internet at http://www.abanes.com/warrensmithmain.html.

8. Gilbert Thurston, "Response to *Deceived on Purpose* by Warren Smith," op. cit.

9. Ibid.

10. Ibid.

11. Richard Abanes, "Warren Smith: Still Self-Deceived on Purpose," (http://www.abanes.com/warrensmith_morelies.html).

12. Tamara Hartzell, *In the Name of Purpose: Sacrificing Truth on the Altar of Unity* (Philadelphia, PA: Xlibris, 2007, to order: 1-888-795-4274), p. 237; citing Alice Bailey & Djwhal Khul, *Problems of Humanity*, (http://

laluni.helloyou.ws/netnews/bk/problems/prob1062.html), Chapter V: "The Problem of the Churches."

13. Dr. Harry Ironside, "Exposing Error: Is it Worthwhile?" (Article posted on The Berean Call website: http://www.thebereancall.org/node/6640).

14. Amy Sullivan, "Rick Warren's Magazine: A Publishing Leap of Faith" (*TIME* magazine, March 10, 2009, http://www.time.com/time/nation/article/0,8599,1884038,00.html p.2), quoting Alyce Alston.

15. Robert H. Schuller, *Prayer: My Soul's Adventure With God: A Spiritual Autobiography* (Nashville, TN: Thomas Nelson, Inc., 1995), front pages, endorsement by Bernie Siegel.

16. Robert H. Schuller, *Believe in the God Who Believes in You* (Nashville, TN: Thomas Nelson, Inc., 1989), p. 247.

17. Gilbert Thurston, "Response to *Deceived on Purpose* by Warren Smith," op. cit.

18. Ibid.

19. Dave Hunt and T.A. McMahon, *The Seduction of Christianity: Spiritual Discernment in the Last Days* (Eugene, OR: Harvest House, 1985), p. 153, citing Robert Schuller from his address at Unity Village; Unity tape.

20. Robert H. Schuller, "Trust for the Crust" (*Hour of Power*, message #1998 delivered 5/18/08, http://www.crystalcathedral.org/hour_of_power/messages/detail.php?contentid=2921).

3/The New Age Peale Factor

1. George D. Exoo and John Gregory Tweed, "Peale's Secret Source" (*Lutheran Quarterly: A Journal for the Evangelical Lutheran Church*, Vol. IX, No. 2, Summer 1995, Marquette University, Milwaukee, Wisconsin), sent by Pastor Larry DeBruyn, Franklin Baptist Church, New Palestine, Indiana.

2. "Norman Vincent Peale Accused of Plagiarism" (*The Indianapolis Star*, August 3, 1995, p. C2), sent by Pastor Larry DeBruyn, author of *Church on the Rise: Why I am not a "Purpose-Driven" Pastor*. To order call 317-897-1298 or go to www.frbaptist.org, Franklin Baptist Church, New Palestine, Indiana.

3. Ibid.

4. George D. Exoo and John Gregory Tweed, "Peale's Secret Source," op. cit.

5. Florence Scovel Shinn, *The Game of Life and How to Play It* (New York, NY: A Fireside Book, Simon & Schuster, Inc., 1986), front and back covers.

6. Norman Vincent Peale, "What Freemasonry Means to Me" (Taken from TRESTLEBOARD, Northwood Ancient-Craft No. 551, http://nac551.com/Masons%2001.08.pdf).

7. Bernie S. Siegel, M.D. *Love, Medicine & Miracles* (New York, NY: Harper & Row Publishers, 1986), back cover.

8. Bernie Siegel, Walsch and the School of the New Spirituality: http:www.schoolofthenewspirituality.com/SNS101BSiegel.cfm.

9. Rhonda Byrne, *The Secret* (New York, NY: Atria Books, 2006), Acknowledgments, p. xv.

10. Neale Donald Walsch, *What God Wants: A Compelling Answer to Humanity's Biggest Question* (New York, NY: Atria Books, 2005), pp. 189-190.

11. Warren Smith, *Deceived on Purpose*, op. cit., pp. 101-102.

12. Ernest Holmes, *The Science of Mind* (New York, NY: Jeremy P. Tarcher/Putnam, First Trade Paperback edition, 1998), back cover.

13. The Oprah Winfrey Show, #W205, Air Date September 18, 1987, official transcript, brought to my attention by Johanna Michaelsen.

14. Eric Butterworth, *Discover the Power Within You: A Guide to the Unexplored Depths Within* (San Francisco, CA: HarperCollins, First HarperCollins Paperback edition, 1992), back cover.

15. Dave Hunt, *Occult Invasion: The Subtle Seduction of the World and Church* (Eugene, OR: Harvest House Publishers, 1998), p. 102; *Possibilities* magazine, Summer 1986, pp. 8-12.

16. "Norman Vincent Peale Accused of Plagiarism," op. cit.

17. Rhonda Byrne, *The Secret*, op. cit., p. 164.

18. Norman Vincent Peale, *The Power of Positive Thinking* (New York, NY: Prentice-Hall, Inc., Sixteenth Printing, 1955), p. 40.

19. Robert H. Schuller, Program #1762, "God's Word: Rebuild, Renew, Restore." (*Hour of Power*, November 9, 2003, http://web.archive.org/web/20031207120013/www.hourofpower.org/booklets/booklets.cfm).

20. Rick Warren, *The Purpose Driven Life*, op. cit., p. 88; citing the *New Century Version* (Dallas, TX: Word Publishers, 1991).

4/George Mair's Book

1. George Mair, *A Life With Purpose: Reverend Rick Warren: The Most Inspiring Pastor of Our Time* (New York, NY: Berkeley Books, 2005), p. 110.

2. Ibid., p. 8.

3. Ibid., p. 9.

4. Ibid., p. 80.

5. Ibid., p. 179.

6. Ibid., p. 93.

7. Ibid., pp. 93-94.

8. Ibid., p. 100.

9. Ibid.

10. Ibid., p. 103.

11. Robert H. Schuller, "What Will Be The Future of This Ministry?" (April 4, 2004, Program #1783, http://www.hourofpower.org.hk/data/readdata100/readeng-129-text.html).

12. George Mair, *A Life With Purpose*, op. cit., p. 110.

13. Ibid., pp. 98-99.

14. Ibid., pp. 192-193.

15. Rick Warren announces his P.E.A.C.E. Plan on November 2, 2003 at Saddleback Church; transcript and audio on file.

16. Lead Like Jesus Celebration, November 20, 2003, Church at Brook Hills in Birmingham, Alabama, online transcript: http://web.archive.org/web/20060208072218/www.bibleoncassette.com/lead_like_Jesus.html.

17. Ibid.

18. Ibid.

19. Lighthouse Trails press release, April 19, 2005, http://www.lighthousetrailsresearch.com/PressReleasekenblanchard.htm.

20. Jim Ballard, *Little Wave and Old Swell: A Fable of Life and its Passing* (Simon & Schuster, 2004), p. vi.

21. Ibid., 2007 edition, pp. 36-37.

22. Ibid., 2004 edition, p. 80.

5/Blaming the Messenger

1. May 31, 2005 e-mail from Rick Warren to Lighthouse Trails Publishing, LLC., http://www.lighthousetrailsresearch.com/emailfromrw.htm, sent at 12:15am.

2. Editors at Lighthouse Trails Publishing, LLC, "Special Report: Rick Warren Teams Up With New-Age Guru Ken Blanchard!" (April 19, 2005, http://www.lighthousetrailsresearch.com/PressReleasekenblanchard.htm).

3. Richard Abanes posted it on AR-Talk (AR-Talk website: http://apologia.org/html/ar_talk.html).

4. May 31, 2005 e-mail from Rick Warren, op. cit.

5. Ibid.

6. Ibid.

7. Ibid.

8. Lead Like Jesus Celebration, November 20, 2003, Church at Brook Hills in Birmingham, Alabama, op. cit.

9. Ken Blanchard, *We Are the Beloved: A Spiritual Journey* (Grand Rapids, MI: Zondervan, 1994), pp. 23-28.

10. SRF Devotee: Connecting SRF Devotees Worldwide: Featured artist Jim Ballard, http://www.srfdevotee.com/featured/spotlite.html.

11. Ken Blanchard, We Are the Beloved, op. cit., p. 95.

12. Ibid.

13. Ray Yungen, A Time of Departing (Silverton, OR: Lighthouse Trails Publishing, LLC, 2nd ed., 2006), chapter 8, "America's Pastor."

14. Deirdre LaNoue, The Spiritual Legacy of Henri Nouwen (New York, NY: Continuum International Publishing Group, 2000), p. 49.

15. Henri Nouwen, Here and Now (New York, NY: The Crossroad Publishing Company, 1997 edition), p. 22.

16. Robert H. Schuller, "God's Word: Rebuild, Renew, Restore," op. cit.

17. Norman Vincent Peale, The Power of Positive Thinking, op. cit., p. 40.

18. Ken Blanchard, We Are the Beloved, op. cit., pp. 65-66.

19. A Course in Miracles: Combined Volume: Text, Workbook for Students, Manual for Teachers (Glen Ellen, CA: Foundation for Inner Peace, 1975, 1992), Text section: p. 147.

20. Ibid., (A Manual for Teachers section), p. 87.

21. Ray Yungen, For Many Shall Come in My Name (Silverton, OR: Lighthouse Trails Publishing, LLC, 2nd edition, 2007), p. 47, citing Neal Vahle, The Unity Movement: Its Evolution and Spiritual Teachings (Radnor, PA: Templeton Foundation Press, 2002, quote by Norman Vincent Peale), p. 423.

22. Ibid., p. 48, citing Marcus Bach, The Unity Way (Unity Village, MO: Unity School of Christianity, 1982), p. 267.

23. May 31, 2005 e-mail from Rick Warren to Lighthouse Trails, op. cit.

24. George Mair, A Life With Purpose, op. cit. p. 93.

25. Robert Schuller, "Trust for the Crust,"op. cit.

26. Robert Schuller, My Journey: From an Iowa Farm to a Cathedral of Dreams (San Francisco, CA: HarperCollins, 2001, First Edition), pp. 227-233; Norman Vincent Peale visited Schuller's drive-in theater church on June 30, 1957.

27. "Who are we?" (Hour of Power, Jubilee Celebration Year; this is no longer on the Hour of Power website but can be accessed at: http://web.archive.org/web/20071122165352/http://www.hourofpower.org/Jubilee/who_are_we.cfm).

28. Warren Smith, Deceived on Purpose, op. cit., p. 113.

29. Editors at Lighthouse Trails, "George Mair's Book: A Life with Purpose" (June 8, 2005, http://www.lighthousetrailsresearch.com/mairwarren.htm); also see: "A Public Response from Lighthouse Trails Publishing" (June 17, 2005, http://www.lighthousetrailsresearch.com/report3.htm).

30. Ibid.

31. A letter sent from George Mair to Lighthouse Trails in 2005 describing these events. On file.

6/Schuller—The *Real* Leader

1. *Hour of Power*, April 24, 2005. Bruce Wilkinson speaking at the Crystal Cathedral. Transcribed by author. No longer available online on *Hour of Power* website. (Note: Some of the actual comments made by Wilkinson in the telecast were changed or omitted from the edited *Hour of Power* online transcript.)

2. Saddleback Church, October 26, 2003. Internet broadcast from Saddleback Church, transcribed by author.

3. Ibid.

4. Warren Smith, *Deceived on Purpose*, op. cit., pp. 121-124.

5. Ibid., pp. 124-126.

6. Source wishes to remain anonymous. On file.

7. This statement was posted on Ken Blanchard's website, but is no longer available; cached file: http://web.archive.org/web/20050808074022/ http://www.leadlikejesus.com/templates/cusleadlikejesus/details. asp?id=21633&PID=89003; for more information on his statement, see: http://www.christianresearchservice.com/KenBlanchard4.htm. For current Ken Blanchard endorsements and updates see: http://www. lighthousetrailsresearch.com/blanchard.htm.

8. Watchman Fellowship; cached file: http://web.archive.org/ web/20061002033957/http://www.watchman.org/blanchardupdate.htm.

9. Blanchard endorsement of Jon Gordon, *The 10-Minute Energy Solution: A Proven Plan to Increase Your Energy, Reduce Your Stress, and Transform Your Life* (New York, NY: Putnam's Sons, 2006), inside front cover. Blanchard's endorsement also sits on Jon Gordon's website: http://www.jongordon.com/012306TheScientificBenefitsofPrayer.htm.

10. For many years, Lead Like Jesus posted a list of their board members on their website. That list is no longer on their site. The following is a cached file from 2004: http://web.archive.org/web/20040718032248/http:// www.leadlikejesus.com/clientImages/21633/nationalboardmembers.htm.

11. Richard Abanes, *Rick Warren and the Purpose that Drives Him* (Eugene, OR: Harvest House, 2005), p. 28.

12. "The Secret To Having Your Best Year Ever," 2008 featuring "the world-renowned stars of *The Secret*," http://web.archive.org/ web/20071228203454/http://yourbestyearever.org, presented by the

Jenna Druck Foundation: http://www.yourbestyearever.org.

13. Jon Gordon, *The No Complaining Rule* (Hoboken, NJ: Wiley & Sons, 2008), front cover.

14. The Hoffman Institute: http://www.hoffmaninstitute.org/about/directors-advisors/advisors.html.

15. Tim Laurence, *The Hoffman Process* (New York, NY: Bantam Dell, Bantam Dell paperback edition, 2004), pp. 206-209.

16. Radio interview with Ken Blanchard, The Call-91.7 WMKL Miami, Florida, http://www.callfm.com. On file.

7/Bernie Siegel Revisited

1. Robert H. Schuller, *Believe in the God Who Believes in You* (New York, NY: Bantam Books, 1989, 1991), pp. 199-200.

2. Bernie S. Siegel, M.D. *Love, Medicine & Miracles* (New York, NY: HarperCollins Publishers, 1986), pp. 18-20.

3. Schuller, *Believe in the God Who Believes in You*, op. cit., pp. 199-200.

4. Robert H. Schuller, "Principles for Powerful, Prosperous Living"-Part IX (*Hour of Power*, Program #1572, no specified date given, http://web.archive.org/web/20050421161228/http://www.hourofpower.org/booklets/archives/pppl_1563-1573/1572.html).

5. Gilbert Thurston, "Response to *Deceived on Purpose* by Warren Smith," op. cit., p. 4.

6. Richard Abanes, *Rick Warren and the Purpose that Drives Him*, op. cit., p. 40.

7. Robert H. Schuller, *Prayer: My Soul's Adventure With God* (Nashville, TN: Thomas Nelson, Inc., 1995), p. ii.

8. Rick Warren, *The Purpose Driven Church*, op. cit., pp. 11-12.

9. Rick Warren's doctoral thesis outline: "New Churches for a New Generation: Church Planting to Reach Baby Boomers. A Case Study: The Saddleback Valley Community Church (California)," 1993 at Fuller Theological Seminary, available on Deception in the Church website: http://www.deceptioninthechurch.com/addendumNAR.html.

10. C. Peter Wagner, *Churchquake: how the new apostolic reformation is shaking up the church as we know it* (Ventura, CA: Regal Books: A Division of Gospel Light, 2000 paperback edition), p. 177.

11. Richard Abanes, *Rick Warren and the Purpose that Drives Him*, op. cit., p. 29.

12. May 31, 2005 e-mail from Rick Warren to Lighthouse Trails Publishing, LLC, op. cit.

13. *The Tides of Change* (A 1995 audio presentation with Rick Warren and Leonard Sweet that was part of an ongoing series called "Choice Voices for Church Leadership," distributed by Abington Press).

14. Rick Warren, *The Purpose Driven Life*, op. cit., dedication, p. 5.

15. Gilbert Thurston, "Response to *Deceived on Purpose* by Warren Smith," op. cit.

16. Tim Stafford, "A Regular Purpose Driven Guy" (*Christianity Today*, November 18, 2002, Vol. 46, No. 12, http://www.christianity today. com/ct/2002/november18/1.42.html).

17. Richard Abanes, *Rick Warren and the Purpose that Drives Him*, op. cit., pp. 99-106.

18. Robert Schuller, *My Journey: From an Iowa Farm to a Cathedral of Dreams*, op. cit., p. 228.

19. Rick Warren, *The Purpose Driven Church*, op. cit., p. 190.

20. Ibid., p. 38.

21. Rick Warren, *The Purpose Driven Church*, op. cit., p. 40 and in various other printings through at least 2008.

22. Richard Abanes, *Rick Warren and the Purpose that Drives Him*, op. cit., p. 103.

23. Kenny Luck, *Dream Workbook* (Colorado Springs, CO: Waterbrook Press, 2007), pp. 131-132.

24. 2002 Institute for Successful Church Leadership, Lee Strobel, http://web.archive.org/web/20021218093027/www.crystalcathedral. org/rhsi/rhsi.speakers.html.

25. For more information on the 2008 Rethink Conference, visit: http:// www.lighthousetrailsresearch.com/rethink.htm. For cached file of 2008 conference speakers, see: http://web.archive.org/web/20080213010558/ www.rethinkconference.com/content/blogcategory/3/14.

26. Gilbert Thurston, "Response to *Deceived on Purpose* by Warren Smith," op. cit.

27. Ibid.

28. Richard Abanes, "Warren Smith, the New Age, and Deception," op. cit..

29. Ibid.

30. Warren Smith, "Rethinking Robert Schuller" (*WorldNetDaily*, October 30, 2007, http://worldnetdaily.com/news/article.asp?ARTICLE_ ID=58409).

31. Robert H. Schuller, *Don't Throw Away Tomorrow: Living God's Dream for Your Life* (New York, NY: HarperCollins, 2005), p. 153.

32. *Hour of Power*, October 17, 2004, Robert H. Schuller's interview with Jerry Jampolsky. (This comment made by Schuller was in the televised interview but did not make it into their written transcript.)

8/"God's Dream": A Deceptive Scheme?

1. Robert H. Schuller, *Self-Esteem: The New Reformation* op. cit., p. 104.

2. Rick Warren, Saddleback Church e-mail, October 27, 2003, GOD'S DREAM FOR YOU–AND THE WORLD!, op. cit.

3. Ann Oldenburg, "The Divine Miss Winfrey" (*USA Today*, May 10, 2006, http://www.usatoday.com/life/people/2006-05-10-oprah_x.htm).

4. Brian McLaren, *Everything Must Change: Jesus, Global Crises, and a Revolution of Hope* (Nashville, TN: Thomas Nelson, 2007), p. 4.

5. Rick Warren, *The Purpose Driven Church*, op. cit., p. 190.

6. Robert H. Schuller, *Your Church Has Real Possibilities* (Glendale, CA: Regal Books Division, G/L Publications, 1974), pp. 176-179.

7. Ibid., p. 179.

8. Robert Schuller, *My Journey: From an Iowa Farm to a Cathedral of Dreams*, op. cit., p. 228.

9. Robert H. Schuller, *Your Church Has Real Possibilities*, op. cit., p. 178.

10. Florence Scovel Shinn, *The Game of Life & How to Play It*, op. cit., (Peale's endorsement of this book is on the back covers of a number of different editions).

11. Neale Donald Walsch, *What God Wants: A Compelling Answer to Humanity's Biggest Question* (New York, NY: Atria Books, 2005), p. 189.

12. Norman Vincent Peale, *The Power of Positive Thinking* (New York, NY: Simon & Schuster, First Fireside Edition, 2003), p. 55. Actual quote reads: "1) PRAYERIZE, 2) PICTURIZE, 3) ACTUALIZE"

13. Rick Warren, *The Purpose Driven Church*, op. cit., p. 190.

14. Warren Smith, *Deceived on Purpose*, op. cit., pp. 104-105.

15. Rick Warren, Saddleback Church e-mail, October 27, 2003, GOD'S DREAM FOR YOU–AND THE WORLD!, op. cit.

16. Warren Smith, *Deceived on Purpose*, pp. 124-125.

17. Gilbert Thurston, "Response to *Deceived on Purpose* by Warren Smith," op. cit.

18. Richard Abanes, "Warren Smith: Still Self-Deceived on Purpose," op. cit.

19. Tim Stafford, "A Regular Purpose Driven Guy" (*Christianity Today*, November 18, 2002, Vol. 46, No. 12, http://www.christianitytoday.com/ct/2002/012/1.42.html).

20. Robert Schuller, *Your Church Has Real Possibilities*, op. cit., p. 6.

21. Ibid., p. 179.

22. Brian McLaren, *The Secret Message Of Jesus: Uncovering the Truth That Could Change Everything* (Nashville, TN: W. Publishing Group, a Division of Thomas Nelson, Inc., 2006), p. 142.

23. Neale Donald Walsch, *Tomorrow's God,: Our Greatest Spiritual Challenge* (New York, NY: Atria Books, 2004), p. 262.

24. See: http://www.thepeacealliance.org.

25. Wayne Dyer, *You'll See It When You Believe It: The Way to Your Personal Transformation* (New York, NY: HarperCollins, First Quill Ed., 2001), p. 108.

26. Ibid., p. 109.

27. Ibid., p. 110.

28. Robert Schuller, *Self-Esteem: The New Reformation*, op. cit., p. 112.

29. Kenny Luck, *Dream: Have You Caught God's Vision?* (Colorado Springs, CO: WaterBrook Press, 2007), p. 146.

30. Luck, *Dream Workbook: Have You Caught God's Vision?*, op. cit., pp. 5-6.

31. Ibid., p. 17.

32. Ibid., p. 142.

33. Ann Oldenburg, "The Divine Miss Winfrey," op. cit.

34. Quote from movie *Field of Dreams*, 1989, Universal City Studios, Inc.

Chapter 8 Sidebar: Who's Talking About "God's Dream"?

1. Robert Schuller, *Don't Throw Away Tomorrow* (San Francisco, CA: HarperCollins, 2005), p. 36.

2. Rick Warren, Saddleback Church e-mail, October 27, 2003, GOD'S DREAM FOR YOU–AND THE WORLD!, op. cit.

3. Erwin McManus, *Wide Awake: The Future is Waiting For You* (Nashville, TN: Thomas Nelson, 2008), p. 179.

4. Bruce Wilkinson, *The Dream Giver* (Sister, OR: Multnomah Publishers, Inc, 2003), p. 77.

5. Shane Claiborne, *Jesus for President* (Grand Rapids, MI: Zondervan, 2008), p. 307.

6. Leonard Sweet, *SoulTsunami, Sink or Swim in the New Millennium Culture* (Grand Rapids, MI: Zondervan, 1999), p. 34.

7. Brian McLaren, *The Secret Message of Jesus*, op. cit., p. 161.

8. Sri Chinmoy (late resident Indian guru at the United Nations, http://www.yogaofsrichinmoy.com/god_the_author_of_all_good/mangod).

9. Desmond Tutu, "Archbishop Desmond Tutu Speech" (March 18, 2004, Bender Arena at American University, http://www1.media.american.edu/speeches/desmondtutu.htm).

10. Sun Myung Moon Speaks on New Morning of Glory (January 22, 1978, http://www.unification.net/1978/780122.html; information courtesy of Discernment Ministries, "A Global Kingdom Dream," http://www.crossroad.to/articles2/08/discernment/8-5-dream-peace.htm).

11. Wayne Dyer, *You'll See it When You Believe It*, op. cit., p. 96.

12. Ann Oldenburg, "The Divine Miss Winfrey," op. cit.

9/Rick Warren and Prophecy Revisited

1. Rick Warren, *The Purpose Driven Life*, op. cit, pp. 285-286.

2. Brian D. McLaren, *The Secret Message of Jesus*, op. cit., p. 171.

3. Rick Warren's doctoral thesis outline, op. cit.

4. C. Peter Wagner, *Churchquake*, op. cit., p. 177.

5. Ibid., pp. 70-71.

6. Robert H. Schuller, *Self-Esteem: The New Reformation*, op. cit., p. 174.

7. Alice A. Bailey, *The Reappearance of the Christ* (New York, NY: Lucis Publishing Company, 1948, Eleventh Printing, 1996), p. 188.

8. Brian McLaren's Everything Must Change Tour, Goshen College May 9-10, 2008; Report by Jeffrey Whitaker, "How 'Everything Must Change,'" http://herescope.blogspot.com/2008/06/how-everything-must-change.html; Tony Jones, *The New Christians: Dispatches From The Emergent Frontier* (San Francisco, CA: Jossey-Bass, 2008), p. 98.

9. Brian D. McLaren, *Everything Must Change*, op. cit., p. 144.

10. Brian McLaren, *The Secret Message Of Jesus*, op. cit., pp. 140-142.

11. Lead Like Jesus Celebration, November 20, 2003, op. cit.

12. Brian McLaren, *The Secret Message of Jesus*, op. cit., p. 142.

13. Brian D. McLaren, *More Ready Than You Realize: Evangelism as Dance In The Postmodern Matrix* (Grand Rapids, MI: Zondervan, 2002), p. 186.

14. Brian McLaren, *Everything Must Change*, op. cit., p. 48.

15. Ibid., p. 52.

10/Warren, Sweet, and Sweet's "New Light" Heroes

1. Leonard Sweet, *Quantum Spirituality: A Postmodern Apologetic* (Dayton, OH: Whaleprints for SpiritVenture Ministries, Inc. 1991, 1994), p. 125.

2. Rick Warren and Leonard Sweet, *The Tides of Change*, op. cit, introductory information sheet.

3. Ibid.

4. Tony Jones, *The New Christianity*, op. cit., pp. 2, 40; Brian McLaren, *Everything Must Change*, op. cit., p. 296; Leonard Sweet, *Quantum*

Spirituality, op. cit., p. viii.

5. Rick Warren and Leonard Sweet, *The Tides of Change*, op. cit.

6. Faith Forward conference in 2007 at Crystal Cathedral with Leonard Sweet, http://www.cathedralgifts.com/20fafoco.html.

7. For information on the small-group workshop at the 2008 Saddleback Small Groups conference: http://www.lighthousetrailsresearch.com/blog/index.php?p=988&more=1&c=1.

8. Leonard Sweet, *Quantum Spirituality*, op. cit., p. viii.

9. Ibid., p. ix.

10. Ibid., p. viii.

11. Marilyn Ferguson, *The Aquarian Conspiracy: Personal and Social Transformation in the 1970s* (Los Angeles, CA: J. P. Tarcher, Inc. 1980), p. 420.

12. Ibid., p. 27.

13. Willis Harman, PH.D, *Global Mind Change: The New Age Revolution In The Way We Think* (New York, NY: Warner Books, 1988), front cover.

14. Leonard Sweet, *Quantum Spirituality*, op. cit., p. 218.

15. Willis Harman, *Global Mind Change*, op. cit., p. 88.

16. Unpublished paper containing quotes from several posts at http://herescope.blogspot.com, used with permission.

17. Warren Smith, "Sign of the Times: Evangelicals and New Agers Together" (*SCP Journal*, 1995); posted at http://www.erwm.com/EvangelicalsandNewAgers.htm.

18. David Spangler, *Emergence: The Rebirth of the Sacred* (New York, NY: Dell Publishing Co., Inc., 1984), p. 80.

19. Ibid., pp. 90-91.

20. Mike Oppenheimer, "A NEW Anointing-Pentecost" (Let Us Reason Ministries, http://www.letusreason.org/Current66.htm).

21. Matthew Fox, *The Coming of the Cosmic Christ: The Healing of Mother Earth and the Birth of a Global Renaissance* (San Francisco, CA: Harper & Row Publishers, 1988), p. 137.

22. Ibid., p. 154.

23. Matthew Fox, *Original Blessing: A Primer in Creation Spirituality Presented in Four Parts, Twent-six Themes and Two Questions* (New York, NY: Jeremy P. Tarcher/Putnam, First Jeremy P. Tarcher/Putnam Edition, 2000), p. 316.

24. Leonard Sweet, *Quantum Spirituality*, op. cit., p. 106.

25. Matthew Fox, *The Coming of the Cosmic Christ*, op. cit., p. 129.

26. Ibid., p. 77.

27. Leonard Sweet, *Quantum Spirituality*, op. cit., p. 124.

28. Ibid., p. 324.

29. Ibid., p. 124.

30. Ibid., p. 324.

31. Ibid., p. 125.

32. Ibid.

33. Rick Warren, *The Purpose Driven Life*, op. cit, p. 88.

34. Pierre Teilhard de Chardin, *Christianity and Evolution* (New York, NY: Harcourt Brace Jovanovich, Inc., 1971), p. 56.

35. One example of where Rick Warren says this is at the Pew Forum of Religion on May 23, 2005, "Myths of the Modern Megachurch," http://pewforum.org/events/index.php?EventID=80. Rick Warren: "You know, 500 years ago, the first Reformation with Luther and then Calvin, was about beliefs. I think a new reformation is going to be about behavior. The first Reformation was about creeds; I think this one will be about deeds. I think the first one was about what the church believes; I think this one will be about what the church does."

36. Robert H. Schuller, *Hour of Power*, "God's Word: Rebuild, Renew, Restore," op. cit.

37. "Myths of the Modern Megachurch," Pew Forum on Religion, op. cit.

38. M. Scott Peck, *The Road Less Traveled* (New York, NY: Simon & Schuster, 1978), p. 281.

39. Ibid.

40. M. Scott Peck, *The Different Drum* (New York, NY: Simon & Schuster, First Touchstone Edition, 1988), p. 17.

41. Ibid., p. 18.

42. Ibid., pp. 18-19.

43. Warren Smith, "M. Scott Peck: Community and the Cosmic Christ" (*SCP Journal*, 19: 2/3), pp. 27-28.

44. Matthew Fox, *The Coming of the Cosmic Christ*, citing endorsement by Peck on back cover.

45. M. Scott Peck, *The Different Drum*, op. cit., pp. 205-206.

46. Leonard Sweet, *Quantum Spirituality*, op. cit., p. 106.

47. Teilhard de Chardin, *Christianity and Evolution*, op. cit., pp. 219-220.

48. Ibid., p. 130.

49. Ibid., p. 95.

50. Jack Canfield and Mark Victor Hansen, *Chicken Soup for the Soul: 101 Stories to Open the Heart and Rekindle the Spirit* (Deerfield Beach,

FL: Health Communications, Inc., 1993), p. 1.

51. Bernie Siegel, *Love, Medicine & Miracles*, op. cit., p. 186.

52. Marianne Williamson, "A New Movement for Peace," speech given April 7, 2002 at the Toledo, Ohio Peace and Justice Conference.

53. Robert H. Schuller, *Don't Throw Away Tomorrow: Living God's Dream for Your Life*, op. cit., p. 183.

11/Sweet, Spangler, and Quantum Spirituality

1. David Spangler and William Irwin Thompson, *Reimagination of the World: A Critique of the New Age, Science, and Popular Culture* (Sante Fe, NM: Bear & Company Publishing, 1991), p. 62.

2. Leonard Sweet, *Quantum Spirituality*, op. cit., p. 312.

3. Ibid., p. ix.

4. See: http://www.clairvoyantguide.com/background.htm.

5. David Spangler, *The Revelation: Birth of a New Age* (Elgin, IL: Lorian Press, 1976), p. 177.

6. Leonard Sweet, *Quantum Spirituality*, op. cit., p. 338, #42.

7. Ibid., p. 48.

8. Ibid., p. 312.

9. Spangler and Thompson, *Reimagination of the World*, op. cit., p. 62.

10. Leonard Sweet, *Quantum Spirituality*, op. cit., p. 113; Spangler and Thompson, *Reimagination of the World*, op. cit., p. 56.

11. M. Scott Peck, *A World Waiting to be Born: Civility Rediscovered* (New York, NY: Bantam Books, 1993), p. 362.

12. Brian McLaren, *Finding Our Way Again: The Return of the Ancient Practices* (Nashville, TN: Thomas Nelson, Inc., 2008), pp. 5-6.

13. Leonard Sweet, *Quantum Spirituality*, op. cit., p. 113.

14. Ibid., p. 13.

15. Spangler and Thompson, *Reimagination of the World*, op. cit., p. 139.

16. Ibid., pp. 139-140.

17. Ibid., p. 140.

18. Leonard Sweet, *Quantum Spirituality*, op. cit., p. 124.

19. "Jan 07: The 50 Most Influential Christians in America" (*Church Report*, January 2007, Online Edition; Sweet ranked #8 of the top 50 listed, http://web.archive.org/web/20071218171701/http://www.thechurchreport.com/mag_article.php?mid=875&mname=January)

20. Leonard Sweet: *SoulTsunami*, op. cit., front cover.

21. Ibid., p. 34.

22. Ibid., p. 17.

23. Matthew Fox, *A New Reformation: Creation Spirituality and the Transformation of Christianity* (Rochester, VT: Inner Traditions, 2006), p. 63.

24. For more information on this small-group workshop, read "2008 Saddleback Small Groups Conference Brings Together Rick Warren and Leonard Sweet" at: http://www.lighthousetrailsresearch.com/blog/index.php?p=988&more=1&c=1.

25. Publicity for small group workshop; Saddleback brochure for this event no longer online.

26. Leonard Sweet, *Quantum Spirituality*, op. cit., p. 148.

27. Richard Abanes, "Leonard Sweet, Rick Warren, and the New Age," http://abanes.com/warren_sweet.html.

28. Richard Abanes and H. Wayne House, *The Less Traveled Road and the Bible: A Scriptural Critique of the Philosophy of M. Scott Peck* (Camp Hill, PA: Horizon Books, 1995), pp. 28-29.

29. Ibid., pp. 2-3.

30. Lead Like Jesus Celebration, November 20, 2003, Church at Brook Hills in Birmingham, Alabama. op. cit.

31. "Lead Like Jesus Revolution" took place in 2008 on October 17th, http://www.leadlikejesus.com/img/c/f185490/Revolution-Speakers.pdf.

32. Brian D. McLaren, *The Secret Message of Jesus*, op. cit., pp. 142-143.

33. Erwin McManus, *An Unstoppable Force: Daring to Become the Church God had in Mind* (Loveland, CO: Group Publishing, 2001), p. 102.

34. Neale Donald Walsch, *Tomorrow's God: Our Greatest Spiritual Challenge* (New York, NY: Atria Books, 2004), p. 56.

35. Neale Donald Walsch, *What God Wants: A Compelling Answer to Humanity's Biggest Question* (New York, NY: Atria Books, 2005), p. 232.

36. Marianne Williamson, *The Gift of Change: Spiritual Guidance for a Radically New Life* (San Francisco, CA: HarperSanFrancisco, 2004), p. 199.

37. Warren Smith, *Deceived on Purpose*, op. cit., p. 132; Brian McLaren, *Finding Our Way Again* (Nashville, TN: Thomas Nelson, 2008), p. 145.

38. Brian McLaren, *Everything Must Change: Jesus, Global Crises, and a Revolution of Hope* (Nashville, TN: Thomas Nelson, 2007).

39. Neale Donald Walsch, *When Everything Changes, Change Everything: In a Time of Turmoil, a Pathway to Peace* (Charlottesville, VA: Hampton Roads Publishing, 2009). For information on Marianne Williamson's Peace Alliance, see http://www.thepeacealliance.org.

12/Fractals, Chaos Theory, Quantum Spirituality, and *The Shack*

1. William P. Young, *The Shack: Where Tragedy Confronts Eternity* (Newbury Park, CA: Windblown Media, 2007), p. 129.

2. The Matrix @ dragoncourt.net (http://www.dragoncourt.net/06.html)

3. William P. Young, *The Shack*, op. cit., p. 112.

4. Rick Warren, *The Purpose Driven Life*, op. cit., p. 88.

5. Warren Smith, *"The Shack* and its New Age Leaven"* (posted at: http://herescope.blogspot.com/2008/06/shack-its-new-age-leaven.html).

6. Jennifer Pekich, "Fractal Theory in *The Shack*" (unpublished article; used with author's permission), quoting in part from: *The Shack*, op. cit., p. 129.

7. Referring to Pastor Larry DeBruyn, Franklin Road Baptist Church: http://www.frbaptist.org.

8. "Fractal Chaos Crashes the Wall between Science and Religion," http://www.fractalwisdom.com.

9. Rick Warren, *The Purpose Driven Life*, op. cit., p. 248, quoted in: Warren Smith, *Deceived on Purpose*, op. cit., pp. 108-109.

10. "Fractal Chaos Crashes the Wall Between Science and Religion," (Fractal Wisdom website, http://www.fractalwisdom.com/FractalWisdom/index.html), quoting Aldous Huxley.

11. Ibid.

12. Ibid.

13. William P. Young, *The Shack*, op. cit., p. 138.

14. Ibid., p. 112.

15. For a more complete explanation of separation versus oneness see Chapter 9, "The 'New Gospel' Doctrine of Separation" in *Reinventing Jesus Christ: The New Gospel* at http://www.deceivedonpurpose.com.

16. Monica Tarantino & Eduardo Araia-Part 2 of 3, an interview with Bruce H. Lipton, Ph.D. (http://spiritcrossing.org/index.php?option=com_content&task=view&id=550&itemid=0).

17. Ibid.

18. David Spangler and William Irwin Thompson, *Reimagination of the World*, op. cit., p. 62.

19. Leonard Sweet, *Quantum Spirituality*, op. cit., p. 312, #86.

20. Rick Warren's endorsement of Bob Buford's book *Halftime* sits on the 2nd page of endorsements inside the front cover of *Halftime* (Grand Rapids, MI: Zondervan, 1994). For more information about the role Buford and the Leadership Network have played in bringing the New

Spirituality into the church, read *Faith Undone: the emerging church—a new reformation or an end-time deception* by Roger Oakland (Silverton, OR: Lighthouse Trails Publishing, 2007), chapter 2; also see Discernment Research Group at http://herescope.blogspot.com.

21. For "Exploring Off the Map" information at Leadership Network's website: http://www.leadnet.org/epubarchive.asp?id=30&db=archive_explorer; also see: "Earth: the Old Story, the New Story" by Discernment Research Group for documentation on the "Exploring Off the Map" conference: Kjos Ministries, http://www.crossroad.to/articles2/08/discernment/5-29-earth-newstory.html.

22. Global Renaissance Alliance, edited by Marianne Williamson, *Imagine: what America Could Be in the 21st Century* (Rodale, Inc, 2000), Margaret Wheatley's chapter titled, "The Future."

23. Margaret J. Wheatley, *Leadership and the New Science: Discovering Order in a Chaotic World* (San Francisco, CA: Berrett-Koehler Publishers, 2006), p. ix.

24. Ibid., pp. ix-x.

25. Ibid., p. xi.

26. Ibid., p. xiii.

27. Ibid.

28. Ibid., pp. 3-4.

29. Brian McLaren, *The Church on the Other Side* (Grand Rapids, MI: Zondervan, 2000 edition), p. 19.

30. Ibid. p. 20.

31. Ibid.

32. Ibid., p. 21.

33. "Off the Map" conference; see footnote #21 of this chapter.

34. Lynn D. Leslie, Sarah H. Leslie and Susan J. Conway, *The Pied Pipers of Purpose: Part 1: Human Capital Systems and Church Performance* (Ravenna, OH: Conscience Press, 2004, http://www.discernment-ministries.org/PDF/Purpose_Driven.pdf), pp. 27-29. ; also see chapter 2 of *Faith Undone* by Roger Oakland, op. cit.

35. Bruce H. Lipton, Ph.D., *The Biology of Belief: Unleashing the Power of Consciousness, Matter & Miracles* (Carlsbad, CA: Hay House Inc., 2008 edition), p. 91; book referred by Pastor Larry DeBruyn.

36. William P. Young, *The Shack*, op. cit., p. 248.

37. Ibid., pp. 129, 138.

38. Ibid., p. 132.

39. Ibid., p. 95.

40. Lead Like Jesus Celebration, November 20, 2003, Church at Brook Hills in Birmingham, Alabama, op. cit.

41. Rick Warren, Saddleback Church e-mail, October 27, 2003, GOD'S DREAM FOR YOU–AND THE WORLD!, op. cit.

42. Brian McLaren, *The Secret Message of Jesus*, op. cit., p. 142; Shane Claiborne, *Irresistible Revolution: Living as an Ordinary Radical* (Grand Rapids, MI: Zondervan, 2006), p. 358; Erwin Raphael McManus, *An Unstoppable Force: daring to become the church God had in mind* (Group Publishing, 2001), p. 102.

43. Rick Warren, *The Purpose Driven Life*, op. cit., p. 286.

44. Quote from movie *Field of Dreams*, op. cit.

45. Alice A. Bailey, *The Reappearance of the Christ* (New York, New York: Lucis Publishing Company), Conclusion, p. 188.

46. Warren Smith, *Reinventing Jesus Christ*, Chapter 4; Smith, *Deceived on Purpose*, Chapters 4, 12, 14. See author's website: http://www.deceivedonpurpose.com for online edition of *Reinventing Jesus Christ*.

47. Ray Yungen, *A Time of Departing*, 2nd ed, Fourth Printing, op. cit., p. 145; citing Rick Warren, *The Purpose Driven Church*, op. cit., p. 126.

48. Henri J.M. Nouwen, *Thomas Merton: Contemplative Critic* (San Francisco, CA: Harper & Row Publishers, 1991, Triumph Books Edition), p. 46, quoting Thomas Merton. Richard Foster includes Thomas Merton's writings in several of his own books, such as *Devotional Classics, Spiritual Classics, Prayer: Finding the Heart's True Home* and others.

49. M. Basil Pennington, *Centered Living* (New York, NY: Image Books, 1988), p. 192. Foster quotes or references Basil Pennington in a number of his books, including *Prayer: Finding the Heart's True Home, Celebration of Discipline*, and *Spiritual Classics*.

50. Ray Yungen, *A Time of Departing*, 2nd ed, Fourth Printing, op. cit., p. 145; citing Rick Warren, *The Purpose Driven Church*, op. cit., p. 126.

51. Tilden Edwards, *Spiritual Friend* (New York, NY: Paulist Press, 1980), p. 18.

52. Leonard Sweet, *SoulTsunami*, op. cit., p. 34.

53. Ibid., p. 109.

54. Richard and Iona Miller, "As Above; So Below: The Mysteries of Quantum Metaphysics" (The Asklepia Foundation, 2001, http://www.geocities.com/nwbotanicalsl/oak/newphysics/asabove.html?200820).

55. Donald J. De Gracia, "Beyond The Physical: A Synthesis of Science and Occultism In Light of Fractals, Chaos, and Quantum Theory" (http://www.geocities.com/octanolboy/bpweb/BP_Index.htm).

56. Ibid.

57. Leonard Sweet, Brian McLaren, Jerry Haselmayer, *A is for Abductive: The Language of the Emerging Church* (Grand Rapids, MI: Zondervan, 2003), p. 130.

58. Rodale and Beliefnet, *From the Ashes: A Spiritual Response to the Attack on America* (USA: Rodale Inc. and Beliefnet, Inc., 2001), p. 21.

59. Neale Donald Walsch, *Conversations with God: an uncommon dialogue, book 1* (New York, NY: G. P. Putnam's Sons, First Hardcover Edition, 1996), p. 198.

60. Neale Donald Walsch, *Conversations with God: an uncommon dialogue, book 3* (Charlottsville, Virginia: Hampton Roads Publishing Company, Inc., 1998), p. 350.

61. Neale Donald Walsch, *Conversations with God, book 1*, op. cit., p. 202.

62. Neale Donald Walsch, *Tomorrow's God*, op. cit., p. 311.

63. Neale Donald Walsch, *Friendship with God: an uncommon dialogue* (New York, NY: G.P. Putnam's Sons, 1999), p. 23.

64. William Paul Young, *The Shack*, op. cit., p. 112.

65. Rick Warren, *The Purpose Driven Life*, op. cit., p. 88.

66. Eugene Peterson, *The Message*, op. cit., p. 23.

67. Ibid., p. 409.

68. From William Paul Young's blog: http://www.windrumors.com/30/is-the-story-of-the-shack-trueis-mack-a-real-person/.

69. Ibid., http://www.windrumors.com/?s=enamored.

70. *The Seeker* DVD (20th Century Fox, 2008), transcribed by Larry DeBruyn.

13/The Quantum Leap to a New Age/New Spirituality

1. *What the Bleep Do We Know!?* (20th Century Fox, 2004, http://www.whatthebleep.com),transcribed by author.

2. Leonard Sweet, *SoulTsunami*, op cit., p. 121.

3. David Spangler and William Irwin Thompson, *Reimagination of the World*, op. cit., p. 126.

4. "Saddleback Presidential Civil Forum," August 16, 2008 (see full transcript by CNN: http://www.clipsandcomment.com/2008/08/17/full-transcript-saddleback-presidential-forum-sen-barack-obama-john-mccain-moderated-by-rick-warren).

5. Ibid.

6. Benjamin Creme, *The Reappearance of the Christ and the Masters of Wisdom* (London, England: The Tara Press, 1980), p. 88; see also: Warren Smith, *Deceived on Purpose*, op. cit, p. 156.

7. Alice Bailey, *The Reappearance of the Christ*, op. cit, p. 150; see also: Smith, *Deceived on Purpose*, op. cit., p. 156.

8. Rick Warren, *The Purpose Driven Life*, op. cit., p. 88.

9. Tom Holladay and Kay Warren, *Foundations Participant's Guide: 11 Core Truths to Build Your Life On* (Grand Rapids, MI, Zondervan, 2003), p. 46; see also Smith, *Deceived on Purpose*, op. cit., p. 157.

10. *Hour of Power*, Robert H. Schuller, Program #1762, "God's Word: Rebuild, Renew, Restore,"November 9, 2003, op. cit.

11. Leonard Sweet, *Quantum Spirituality*, op. cit., p. 125.

12. Warren Smith, *Deceived on Purpose*, op. cit, pp. 32-34; Ronald S. Miller and the Editors of *New Age Journal*, *As Above, So Below: Paths to Spiritual Renewal in Daily Life* (Los Angeles, CA: Jeremy P. Tarcher, Inc., 1992), p. xi.

13. Fritjof Capra, *The Tao of Physics: An Exploration of the Parallels between Modern Physics and Eastern Mysticism* (Boston, MA: Shambhala Publications, Inc., 1999), p. 11.

14. Ibid., p. 323.

15. Ibid., pp. 324-325.

16. Ibid., p. 330.

17. Ibid., p. 341.

18. Margaret J. Wheatley, *Leadership and the New Science: Discovering Order in a Chaotic World* (San Francisco, CA: Berrett-Koehler Inc., 3rd ed., 2006), pp. 3-4, brought to my attention by Discernment Research Group.

19. *Emerging Leaders: Relational Foundations of Leadership* (Sioux Falls, SD, Vantage Point[3], 2006, http://www.vantagepoint3.org/fileadmin/main/tour/EMS3%20WebSamples.pdf), p. 52; this information provided by Jennifer Pekich.

20. Annette Capps, *Quantum Faith* (England, AR: Capps Publishing, 2003, 2007), p. 4, booklet brought to my attention by Larry DeBruyn.

21. Ibid., p. 6.

22. Marilyn Ferguson, *The Aquarian Conspiracy*, op. cit., pp. 145, 149-150, 152, 172, 261, 374.

23. Gary Zukav's first appearance on *Oprah* was in October 1998. This propelled his book *The Seat of the Soul* to the top of the *New York Times* best-seller list for two years.

24. *What the Bleep Do We Know!?* transcribed by Warren Smith, op. cit.

25. Ibid.

26. Ibid.,

27. Neale Donald Walsch, *Tomorrow's God*, op. cit, p. 84-85; For more

information on Rick Warren's relationship with Peter Drucker see Lynn D. Leslie, Sarah H. Leslie and Susan J. Conway, *The Pied Pipers of Purpose,* op. cit.

28. Neale Donald Walsch, *Tomorrow's God,* op. cit., pp. 84-85.

29. Kathy Juline, "Question Authority: A Conversation with Neale Donald Walsch," *Science of Mind,* May 2004, p. 29.

30. "Humility Theology" from John Marks Templeton, *The Humble Approach: Scientists Discover God* (Philadelphia, PA: Templeton Foundation Press, 1995).

31. Warren Smith, *Deceived on Purpose,* p. 63; this quote originally taken from the Conversations with God website (http://www.cwg.og); a close rendition of it can be found in Walsch's book *The New Revelations,* op. cit., back cover.

32. Ibid.

33. Ibid.

34. John Marks Templeton, *The Humble Approach,* op. cit., p. 53.

35. Ibid., p. 38.

36. Ibid., p. 46.

37. Ibid., p. 137.

38. Dave Hunt, *Occult Invasion: The Subtle Seduction of the World and the Church* (Eugene, OR: Harvest House Publishers, 1998), p. 102; *Possibilities* magazine, Summer 1986, pp. 8-12.

39. John Marks Templeton, *Discovering the Laws of Life* (New York, NY: The Continuum Publishing Company, 1994), p. 1.

40. Ibid., p. 2.

41. John Heidenry, *Theirs Was the Kingdom,* op. cit., p. 252; book was brought to my attention by Discernment Ministries.

42. Ibid., p. 588; information provided by RDA per telephone call to Reader's Digest Association, Inc.

43. Ibid., p. 252.

44. John Marks Templeton, *Discovering the Laws of Life,* op. cit., p. 70.

45. Gregg Braden, "Are We Passive Observers or Powerful Creators?" (*Evolve!: A Magazine of Evolutionary Products, People, and Ideas,* Volume 6- number 2), p. 5.

46. Rick Warren and Leonard Sweet, *The Tides of Change,* op. cit.

47. Ibid.

48. Rick Warren, Saddleback Church e-mail, October 27, 2003, GOD'S DREAM FOR YOU–AND THE WORLD!, op. cit.

49. Leonard Sweet, *SoulTsunami,* op. cit., p. 55.

50. Ibid.

51. Ibid., p. 34.

52. Ibid., p. 109.

53. Ibid., p. 121.

54. Leonard Sweet, *Quantum Spirituality*, op. cit., p. 106.

55. Richard Abanes, "Leonard Sweet, Rick Warren, and the New Age," http://abanes.com/warren_sweet.html.

56. Leonard Sweet, *So Beautiful* (Colorado Springs, CO: David C. Cook, 2009), p. 279, #118.

57. Ibid., p. 101.

58. Ibid., p. 256, #22.

59. Ibid., p. 278, #107.

60. Rick Warren referred to "Christian fundamentalism" as "one of the big enemies of the 21st century." See: Paul Nussbaum, "The purpose-driven pastor," *Philadelphia Inquirer*, Jan. 08, 2006, http://web.archive.org/web/20060522084523/www.philly.com/mld/inquirer/living/religion/13573441.htm?template=contentModules/printstory.jsp.

On May 23, 2005, Rick Warren spoke at the Pew Forum on Religion and stated the following: "Today there really aren't that many Fundamentalists left; I don't know if you know that or not, but they are such a minority; there aren't that many Fundamentalists left in America. . . . Now the word 'fundamentalist' actually comes from a document in the 1920s called the Five Fundamentals of the Faith. And it is a very legalistic, narrow view of Christianity." See: "Myths of the Modern Megachurch," http://pewforum.org/events/index.php?EventID=80.

14/Rick Warren's "Broad Way" Christianity

1. *TIME* magazine March 10, 2009 Amy Sullivan, http://www.time.com/time/nation/article/0,8599,1884038,00.html p. 1; for more information regarding Rick Warren and the Purpose Driven movement, and related issues, see *Trojan Horse: The New Age Corruption of the Evangelical Faith* by Gregory R. Reid. To order: www.xulonpress.com.

2. Victoria Neufeldt, Editor in Chief, *Webster's New World Dictionary: Third College Edition* (New York: Simon & Schuster, Inc., 1988), p. 445.

3. Rick Warren, *The Purpose Driven Life*, op. cit., p. 203.

Index

O

Obama 163, 164, 165
occult 18-19, 35-36, 39, 40-46, 50, 51, 84, 85, 124, 125, 127, 132, 141-143, 156, 160, 161, 172
Omega Point 111
oneness 43, 133, 134, 145, 148, 154, 159, 169, 170, 173
Oneness 19, 20, 56, 122, 134, 136, 145, 156, 158

P

Pagitt, Doug 150
panentheism 112, 113, 114, 167
pantheism 113, 114
paradigm 110, 169, 178
Paramahansa Yogananda 55, 62, 72
peace and harmony 99
P.E.A.C.E. Plan 24-25, 27, 28, 52-56, 58, 71, 73, 86-89, 92, 102, 154, 179, 180, 185, 191
Peacocke, Arthur 113
Peale, Norman Vincent 12-14, 38-51, 54, 56, 60, 62-67, 69, 70, 76, 78, 84, 85, 91, 142, 150, 176, 177, 178
Peck, M. Scott 106, 107, 115-119, 121, 124, 129, 133, 134, 135
Pennington, Basil 155
perennial wisdom 109
Peterson, Eugene 18, 19, 20, 45, 141, 142, 146, 158, 159, 160, 167,
Popper, Karl 108
positive future 43, 154, 180, 181
Possibilities magazine 22, 44, 175
possibility thinking 12
postcolonial 126
post-enlightenment 126
postmodern 89, 104, 106, 107, 108, 126, 127, 130, 131, 181, 182, 183
Postmodern Reformation 131, 180
Power of Positive Thinking, The 39, 42, 46, 63, 66, 84, 85, 177
Power of Purpose Essay Contest 22, 44, 176
President of the United States 13
preterism 100
prophecy 20, 96, 97, 99, 102, 110, 150, 171, 184
Protestantism 39
psychology and theology 50
Purpose Driven alliances 28

T

U

V

Also by Warren Smith

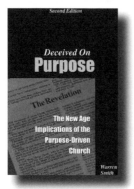

Deceived on Purpose: The New Age Implications of the Purpose Driven Church

Warns about the serious New Age implications of Rick Warren's book *The Purpose Driven Life*. Smith takes the reader into the inner workings of today's evangelical world as he explores the questionable interconnections of several of its top leaders. As Rick Warren goes worldwide with his purpose-driven global P.E.A.C.E. plan, Smith presents an in-depth examination of this mega-church pastor's spiritual agenda. He explains how Rick Warren's Peace plan could eventually merge with the New Age Peace plan that is being similarly presented by key New Age leaders. 212 pages, 2nd edition, $12.95, Softbound. For wholesale orders of this title for 10 or more copies, contact Bookmasters: 800/247-6553.

The Light That Was Dark: From the New Age to Amazing Grace

Warren Smith was a spiritual seeker. That journey led him down a yellow-brick road of pied-piper spirits, landing him in a metaphysical New Age where the Christ proclaimed wasn't the real Christ at all. Following signs and wonders, he jumped through spiritual hoops with almost flawless precision, until one day he realized that the light he was following was not light at all but rather darkness. Concerned that today's church is being seduced by the same false teachings and the same false Christ that drew him into the New Age, Smith shares his story in a most compelling way. 168 pages, 2nd edition, $12.95 Softbound. For wholesale orders of this title, for 10 or more copies, contact Bookmasters: 800/247-6553.

Also by Lighthouse Trails Publishing

BOOKS

A Time of Departing, 2nd ed.
by Ray Yungen, $12.95

Castles in the Sand
by Carolyn A. Greene
$12.95, illustrated, photos

Trapped in Hitler's Hell
by Anita Dittman with Jan Markell
$12.95, illustrated, photos

Out of India
by Caryl Matrisciana
$12.95, illustrated, photos

Another Jesus (2nd Edition)
by Roger Oakland, $12.95

Things We Couldn't Say
1st Lighthouse Trails Edition
by Diet Eman , $14.95

The Other Side of the River
by Kevin Reeves, $12.95

For Many Shall Come in My Name
(2nd Edition)
by Ray Yungen, $12.95

Laughter Calls Me
by Catherine Brown
$12.95, Illustrated, photos

DVDs

Standing Fast in the Last Days
with Warren Smith
$14.95, 57 minutes

The Story of Anita Dittman
with Anita Dittman
$15.95, 60 minutes

The New Face of Mystical Spirituality
with Ray Yungen
3-DVDs, $39.95 or $14.95 ea.

CDs

Good News in the Badlands
with Bob Ayanian
Americana gospel folk music
$16.95, 19 songs

For a complete listing of all our books and DVDs, go to www.lighthousetrails.com, or request a copy of our catalog.

To order additional copies of:

A *"Wonderful" Deception*

Send $14.95 per book plus shipping
($3.95 for 1 book, $5.25 for 2-3 books) to:

Lighthouse Trails Publishing
P.O. Box 958
Silverton, Oregon 97381

For bulk rates of 10 or more copies, contact Lighthouse Trails
Publishing, either by phone, online, e-mail, or fax. You may order
online at www.lighthousetrails.com or
for US orders, call our toll-free number: 866/876-3910.

For international and all other calls: 503/873-9092
Fax: 503/873-3879

A *"Wonderful" Deception* as well as other books by Lighthouse Trails
Publishing, can be ordered through all major outlet stores, bookstores,
online bookstores, and Christian bookstores. Bookstores may order
through: Ingram, SpringArbor or directly through Lighthouse Trails.

Libraries may order through Baker & Taylor.
Quantity discounts available for most of our books.

For more information:
Lighthouse Trails Research Project
www.lighthousetrailsresearch.com

Also visit the author's website:
www.deceivedonpurpose.com